QUOTH THE CANOVA

"Live your life so that you'll be proud to have Don Ameche play it some day!"

"When I get a run in my stocking, I don't know whether I've got a clinker, a splinter, or a blowout!"

ON EGO

"Remember, more people have been flattened by a right to the back than a left to the jaw."

"I have what you call a postwar problem. I've got an over supply of natural resources, but something is wrong with my distribution."

ON A RADIO SCRIPT
SHE DIDN'T THINK WAS FUNNY

"It's not worth the paper it's rotten on."

JUDY CANOVA

SINGIN' IN THE CORN

by Ben Ohmart

Published in the USA by:
BearManor Media
PO Box 1129
Duncan, Oklahoma 73534-1129
www.bearmanormedia.com

ISBN 978-1-59393-316-6

Printed in the United States of America.
Edited by Lon Davis.
Book design by Brian Pearce | Red Jacket Press

Table of Contents

For Diana and Julieta

Foreword

Judy Canova! That sweet little lady who had the gumption of a tomcat mixed with the throat of an opera/Opryland singer, and the style sense of a 30-year-old catalog. She may've been slow, but not rightly stupid. She may've preferred pigtails to ball gowns and a mess o' men to owin' her lonely hearts club dues, but this was a girl with a heart of gold, a jaw of iron, and a head of pure Georgia pine straw.

That's Judy Canova the character, of course, not Judy Canova, the natural comedienne, the flawless, yodeling singer, the loving mother, and perpetual bride. She was as complex as Hollywood in the 1930s and 1940s would allow, if a woman wanted it all. She nearly had it. At the height of her career in films and radio, no one was more respected on the corn-cob circuit than our Judy. Indeed, Judy Canova is and was to the hillbilly style what Coke is to cola.

Film historian James Robert Parish put it beautifully in his book, *Hollywood Songsters*, when he wrote, "It was Judy Canova, in the 1930s-50s, who made hillbilly humor a national pastime through her successful work on the Broadway stage, in films, on recordings, and especially on radio."

Judy worked hard at keeping her image as the anti-styled hick, devoid of any sense save common, and in a big way, she self-perpetuated the stereotype of country star living to the point where people just wouldn't believe her if she stepped out of character. It would be as if Harpo Marx were to go on *The Tonight Show* to talk about his latest film.

The reporter known as Casanova summed it up aptly when he interviewed Judy at her home for the December 1946 issue of *Judge* magazine: "She swung her dainty feet gracefully off the divan and moved over to make room for me. It was then I noticed her colossal GI shoes which she always wears to her NBC broadcasts — an incongruous note since I always visualized hill-william characters as barefooted. However, her corn-cob pipe which she was puffing contentedly gave me a sense of reassurance."

Of course that was all a put-on for the press. People wanted Judy to remain corn-fed and dumb as a cluck. When she appeared out of pigtails and baggy checkered dress, she actually received complaints from *fans*.

She always made the papers with a photo when she frequently appeared at public events, clubs, or on the street wearing her to-the-knee fur coat, hair up, looking more like a starlet than a rube. "One of these days," she said during the filming of *Louisiana Hayride*, "I'm going to break out with some real stylish clothes in a picture. It will probably be an evening outfit consisting of dungarees and a V-back sweater." She knew just what audiences expected of her.

Some articles in 1946 rumored that Judy was starting to pen an autobiography to be called *There's a Punch in Judy*, after hooking up with a New York publisher. Three years later it was reported that she would be writing a book on *all* famous Canovas for Simon & Schuster to be titled *A Collection of Canovas*. Alas, neither was to be.

A few newspaper blurbs had Judy saying that she'd like to call her biography, *The Corn is Grown*. But I think *Singin' in the Corn*, even if it hadn't been the name of one her films, best describes this hollarin' pigtail champ; she of the slack jaw, rolling eyes, tiny cowgirl hat, and concealed glamour.

As influential as she was to her contemporaries (and remembered as she is today to the country music, radio, and classic film crowds), it's rather amazing that no one had heretofore tackled a full-length biography on Judy Canova. Of course even this book would not exist were it not for the bountiful generosity of Judy's two daughters, Diana and Julieta, who loaned me every scrap of memorabilia they had on their mother, not to mention the hours of time they devoted to answering my endless questions. This is *their* book, which I have dedicated to them.

Filling in the many missing holes that cropped up, I have to thank the following people for their tireless, *much* appreciated help: my wife Mayumi, for being so wonderful at every stage of the game: listening, helping, nurturing; Kevin Minton, for supplying many of the film stills you see here, and generally being a good cheerleader — when I can find him!; Jim Parish for writing *all* those books, and giving support to the little guy; Martin Grams, Jr., for answering any question on radio that can ever be thought up; Laura Wagner, for caring so much about film history and proving that there is someone here to preserve old films and their information for the *now* and later generations; Richard Oscar, for supplying some of the more hard-to-find JC films; and Randy Bonneville for an expertly done credit list, just one of many from his *massive* files.

My own love for Judy started with hearing her enchanting radio series. The show had one of the best casts in radio, some of the best writing, and

then there was Judy, singing her heart out, mixing it with unpretentious comedy that never failed to deliver. So...there might be a bit too many quotes from the radio show in this here book, but I do believe that a lot of that corn she fed us is still utterly filling.

It was quite a journey, writing this book. Literally. My wife and I drove up from Georgia to Connecticut to visit Diana and borrow a ton of stuff that is really the heart and bones of this book. Diana made us feel *so* welcome in her beautiful home, giving us homemade banana bread and hot tea on the *very* rainy day we arrived. Her kindness certainly gave me extra motivation to finish this book on such a loveable icon of films.

Diana explained, "I myself am still trying to figure her out. I do know by looking at her old photo album that she was a fun kid when she was young. She knew how to laugh and have a good time. I think that's important to note. And so gifted. I worked with Estelle Parsons and one night we were talking about my mother. She hadn't realized that I was Judy's daughter and when I told her, Estelle said so earnestly, 'Oh honey, she was so *gifted*.' Yep."

In one of the many Canova scrapbooks I borrowed from Diana, between the unlabeled photos, Canova family achievements and odd clippings of news stories, everything from religious poetry to odd science discoveries to little bits ("Chicago — Girl in red sold Dillinger's life for $10,000 blood money") were the occasional handwritten sayings. One was simply:

> *Would you live with ease*
> *Do what you ought*
> *And not what you please.*

If Judy had a philosophy for life, I believe that would sum it up nicely.

Ben Ohmart

CHAPTER ONE

Rube via Venice

The Canova clan originally sprawled from Minorca, Spain and Portugal into Florida. Judy's grandfather, a cattleman, was born in Madrid, and was a descendant of the eminent Italian sculptor and painter, Antonio Canova (1757-1822). Antonio, himself the son of a stone cutter, studied intensively in Rome where he began the first of many commissions for Venetian ambassador Girolamo Zulian, for whom he created *Teseo sul minotauro* (1781-1783). His later works led him to historic fame when he was commissioned to create busts for the Napoleon family, including a large marble statue of Bonaparte in heroic nudity as *Marte Pacificatore* (1803-1806).

Another version of the history had young Antonio sent away by a rich family of Venice to study, at the same time earning money in the kitchen of one of the Venetian princes. This prince liked his food served in fancy form, and that's where Judy's ancestor excelled. "The way I hear it," she told the press, "the regular chef carved a roast to look like a bird, fruit into flowers, and bread into pillars. But one day he got sick. So young Tony took over, carving up his premier meal into a first-class zoo. Complete with a lion from butter. The prince wept with delight when he saw it. I guess Antonio could have had the job regular if he'd wanted it. But he didn't like the idea of his fine work ending up in the prince's stomach. So he stuck to sculpturing.

"He spent his last years designing a burial temple for himself and, relatives, being what they are, this was probably his artistic project the family liked best," she continued. "Anyway, when the finishing touch — Antonio — was laid in the temple, all the Canovas for miles around picked up and moved into his castle."

At the height of Judy's fame, newspapers stated that the star would later inherit that castle. But according to Judy's eldest daughter, Julieta (also known as "Tweeny"), "As far as I know Mom never inherited anything in Italy. I have a feeling that was just PR. The origin of the branch of the family that came to settle in Florida was from Minorca, Spain. I know that the artist Antonio Canova had no children. But he had a brother or half-brother, and it is through the Canova side that the Canovas migrated to Minorca, and then to St. Augustine, Florida. As far as any land in Italy — had she inherited it, we probably would have known about it, as the entire group of siblings would have been arguing, fighting, and bellyaching that it was part theirs as well — as would Viola Clarke's [Judy's cousin] side of the clan. Had she inherited it and sold it, Dee Dee and I would have heard about it *ad nauseum*, as she would have regretted selling it."

Diana (*aka* "Dee Dee"), Judy's youngest daughter, had almost the same answer: "I never heard about an estate in Italy. Somehow I don't think

Mom did either. I'm starting to realize I have very little knowledge about my mother because I might have gotten the studio version and not the real one!"

By the time the first generation of "American" Canovas had truly settled in the St. Augustine, Florida area, it was 1865. George Paul Canova married Diannah Greene that year and established a mercantile store using the thousands of acres his father, Bartolo (also referred to as Paul B. Canova), had acquired before returning to Jacksonville, Florida, to become a steamboat captain. With their parents' money to stake them, George and Diannah eventually became rich, owning a hotel, a cotton gin, a thousand head of cattle, and thousands of acres of orange groves.

The captain was quite a character. The following is an article written by Judge Warren P. Ward, grandson-in-law of the colorful Capt. Canova, which ran in the "Ward's Column" of the *Coffee County Progress* in Douglas, Georgia on December 3, 1935.

> Many years before the War Between the States, one of the largest and oldest commercial business houses in Jacksonville, Florida, was Busbee and Canova. They were wholesale grocers and liquor dealers. The little brick store was located on the corner of Ocean and Bay Street. They did an extensive business up and down the St. John's River and throughout the small towns of the interior. Many country people with wagons and carts came as far as Live Oak, Lake City, Starke, and Gainesville. One habit this firm had was to place a jug of good liquor in every country wagon that came to their place of business. The senior member of this firm was Capt. Paul B. Canova, who was a member of that large and well-known Canova family, reared in St. Augustine, and were leading businessmen in every section of the state. Capt. Paul B. Canova was captain on a steamboat which ran between Jacksonville and Palatka on the St. Johns River.
>
> The old Canova home was situated on the banks of the St. Johns River at the foot of Liberty Street, as well as I remember. Grandmother Canova was a Crespo before she married Capt. Canova. They were high type Spaniards and were all proud of the Crespo name for some member of that family held military offices of distinction. When I married Miss Annie Canova, the eldest grand-daughter of Capt. Canova, I was given a warm welcome into the family and our grandmother Canova was always delighted to tell me much of the

Left to right: Paul Bartola Canova (Father), Celestina Crespo (Mother), George Paul Canova, Diannah Green Canova, Betsy Ann Green, mother of Dinannah Green Canova.

Katherine, (Mother), Adaline, Annie.

Left to right: Albert, Will, Nolan, Lonnie, George, Joe, Ed, Paul, Tom.

family history, and you must not forget that she wanted to know some of *my* family history.

As the years went by we became very fond of each other and many times she has placed her hand on my shoulder and said, "I love you just as much as I do my son, George." One day she and I walked down to the river and she showed me the home where she had lived many years and where she reared a large family. Her oldest son, George Paul Canova, was the only boy. She pointed out to me where the old boat landed and how she watched the river's bend to see her husband, Capt. Paul Canova, as his boat came into sight.

She told me many exciting experiences that Capt. Canova had had as captain on the St. Johns River. They had no pirates on the river to deal with, but they had winds and storms, robbers, and tough men of every character. She told me about a terrible storm they had on the river. They had many bad storms from time to time, but she took time to tell me all about one particular storm. The St. Johns River is a large river; it averages one mile wide for three hundred miles. A storm blowing in from the ocean was terrific. Boats and houses along the river would be demolished. The water would pile up like ocean waves in this big old river and often small boats, dredges and other kinds of water craft would be driven out into the streets and at times like this the river was very dangerous.

Grandmother Canova knew what time of day or night to expect her husband's boat to appear. She had signal lights in her home to place in position in order that Capt. Canova could see them, as he appeared in sight. He also had signal lights on his boat so his family could see his boat in sight. They were all Catholics and believed in making the Sign of the Cross at every approach of danger, so when the storm was raging at its worst, it gave them great satisfaction as each could see the other making the Sign of the Cross.

Capt. Canova also held the office of sheriff of Duval County for many years. During the time he was sheriff, a horrible crime was committed. At a large saw-mill located in the eastern part of the city, a young lady was assaulted and murdered. Under the fine detective work of Capt. Canova, three of the murderers were captured, tried and convicted of the crime, and hanged.

His son George died of "lead poisoning," being the victim of a mysterious shooting that took place while he was riding through wooded country in a buggy. Sensational-sounding news reports of the day wrote that because of the lack of leads or desire for justice by local law enforcement, his nine sons took it upon themselves to promptly and vigorously clean up the community. (The nine sons had a baseball rivalry with the

The nine Canova brothers at the ol' Canova house. Back row: Will, Tom, Albert. Front row: Ed, Joe, Nolan, George (Walter), Lonnie (Alonzo), Paul.

next-door neighbors who also had nine sons.) The killing was never solved, but the district became a safer place.

Diannah and George had been busy raising a family of nine boys and three girls on Monroe Street in the Jacksonville area, where they were all educated and encouraged to become fine musicians. George was Catholic, and very religious, but when his brother-in-law, Thaddeus Hill, converted to the Church of Jesus Christ of Latter-day Saints, George, Diannah (raised Baptist) and their children were soon baptized as Mormons. George Canova would become an elder of his new church by January 1898.

As the press had it, Judy's mother, Henrietta Perry Canova, was British, a descendent of Commodore Perry. Anne Canova, Judy's sister, later told the press, "Our father was in the cotton business and we heard the colored and white people sing [folk music] at work. We pattern our style of singing somewhat after them."

Judy's daughter Julieta stated that "Our grandma — Gogga, or Retta — was born Henrietta Perry Canova. She was a formally trained pianist and mother of eight. She married Joseph Francis Canova, a cotton broker. Judy's father played the banjo and sang at parties in Flor-

The Canova homestead in Jacksonville, Florida.

ida, but didn't really like the idea of his children going on the stage. "Retta was the disciplinarian. Her motto was, 'You don't have to love me but, by God, you will respect me' — never thinking that might be a two-way street. Mom was her baby, the youngest child. And that bond was stronger than any you can imagine. I don't know that it was so much love as it was *fear* on the part of our mother. If you look up the word 'control' in the dictionary, you will probably see Retta's picture. The children who rebelled, i.e., disagreed with her or didn't follow her dictates, were either ostracized, castigated, or chased out the house with a butcher knife (hearsay from our Mammy Alma Lacey, who claimed she was there when it happened). "Retta ruled the house — any house she was in — with an iron fist. She knew how to cook, how to garden, how to can and preserve, make jelly, play poker, and quote Scripture. She played ragtime piano as well as Scott

Joplin, and could put you to sleep with Chopin. She was short and sturdy, and she instilled fear in every child in the family. My mom's sister, Anne, had a daughter — Juliana. My Uncle Pete (Harry) and his wife adopted a daughter — Floretta. Mom's cousin Viola Clarke had a daughter — Karen. And then there was me. Each one of us was scared to death of Gogga and her temper. If you didn't do it (whatever 'it' was) to her exact

Judy's Parents, Joseph Francis Canova and Henrietta (Retta) Perry Canova.

specifications, she would either spank you with her wooden hairbrush or make you go out to the fishpond and cut a 'switch' from the willow tree for a switchin'. And if it wasn't quite right, you had to go cut another one.

"There's at least *one* positive thought about our grandmother I should share. The family had a friend named Lucille Joy. Lucille became housebound as she aged, and she was unable to go to church. She was a Christian and it devastated her that she was unable to go to her church services every Sunday. When Gogga found out Lucille was no longer able to get to church, she started calling Lucille on Sunday mornings. They'd read the Bible together and sing a hymn, say a prayer. It wasn't until after Gogga died that we found out she'd always say, 'Now it's time for the collection.' A couple of days later, Lucille would get a small check from her in the mail. So I guess she wasn't a complete monster.

"Gogga suffered a heart attack before I was born and died from another one when I was five — right after Mom married Diana's dad, Fili. Most of the adults in the family thought the attack was caused by the anger from

Mom running off and marrying him against Retta's will. I don't think she was as educated as she could have been, but ran on native intelligence. And when she realized that Fili had taken her place at the top of the tree, she couldn't take it and didn't have enough of an educational background to be able to figure a way around it. All I remember of her death is that I was walking from the pool house to the main house and could hear my mother

The four Canovas.

screaming and crying. Then all the adults in the family packed off to the funeral in Florida and left us kids (my cousins and me) at home with 'the help.' "Gogga drove cross country (well, she didn't do the driving) with Mom, Pete, Foncie (Pete's wife), Zekie (Uncle Leon — Mom's other brother), Pete's two dogs (standard Schnauzers) from the East Coast to Hollywood when Mom broke into the big time. And one of the stories is that there were a couple of guys flirting with Mom and Anne at a service station (could have been a café), and Gogga said, 'God, this purse is heavy. Must be my gun — got to get a smaller one.' Now, whether she had a firearm in there or not, the guys were not about to test it. Maybe that's where the family acting gene started.

"When they got to Hollywood and Mom made her first picture (with the trio), it was Gogga who decided that Pete, who could play banjo and guitar, would handle the business part, and not perform. Whatever the story really is, there was eventually a rift and since they died within a close time span, the rift was never healed. Family lore is that the reason Pete died of a heart attack was that his heart had been broken because Gogga froze him out of the family. Mom by that time had the radio show, Anne and Zeke were on the payroll, and Pete was left to twist in the wind and really had nothing to do except the bookkeeping and be with his family."

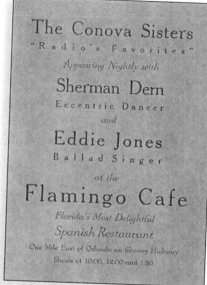

The Conova Sisters
"Radio's Favorites"

Appearing Nightly with

Sherman Dern
Eccentric Dancer

and

Eddie Jones
Ballad Singer

at the

Flamingo Cafe
Florida's Most Delightful
Spanish Restaurant

One Mile East of Orlando on Cheney Highway
Shows at 10:00, 12:00 and 1:30

Left: Little Juliette. Above: Before they were the Canova Trio, it was just Anne and Judy.

Juliette "Judy" Canova was born in Starke, Florida, on November 20, 1913. Some sources state her birthplace as Jacksonville, although Judy herself claimed Unadilla, Georgia, as her hometown for the simple reason that she liked the name. At age 11 she moved to Jacksonville, Florida, where she attended school. It didn't take her long to get on the radio by way of talent contests, winning quite a few for her singing and dancing abilities.

As they were growing up, the young Canova siblings — Anne, Zeke, Judy, and Pete — spent the summers with friends and relatives from the areas of Hendersonville and Asheville, North Carolina, and Douglas, Georgia, where they began to learn the ways of the hillbilly language and its songs. Some early press stories state that the Canovas (occasionally referred to as "The Three Georgia Crackers") came from Douglas, Georgia. Almost, but not quite. One review of a particular performance stated that they "sing just exactly the way they used to back home in Douglas, Georgia, and everything they know they learned from the Negroes who used to work round their father's cotton mill." Judy told newspapers in 1934 that "you couldn't get a real hillbilly to go on the stage. He would be so frightened that he would run away. They don't like strangers and they want to stay right in the mountains."

Performing — especially on the music side — was becoming very important in young Judy's life. She later told a magazine reporter of one of her earliest ventures into showbiz.

> A kid circus was staged in the school gymnasium in Jacksonville. It was one of those highly disorganized affairs where everyone gets to put on his act, and the proud mamas and papas are apt to have a lot more fun than their perspiring offspring.
>
> My specialty, at the time, was a highly nasal rendition of the song that starts out, "I had a dog and his name was Rover. He was a very intelligent pup. He could stand up on his hind legs — if you held his front legs up." The song goes through innumerable verses. That was my number. I was dressed in a clown suit several sizes too large, and wore a pointed cap on top of my pigtails.
>
> When I first stepped out on the gymnasium floor, alone, in that white circle from which the centers start the basketball game, I was petrified. But I warmed up by the end of the first verse, got the quaver out of my voice, and waded triumphantly through the rest of the song. When I finished, there was applause and laughter, and those were the sweetest sounds I ever heard. I guess I was a goner for show business from that instant.

It seems she was born with those pigtails. It also turned out that Judy was a natural-born contortionist, having learned the moves from dancing. She stated, "Mother got alarmed watching me sitting on my own head. Couldn't see what future there was in that, so she took me back home to school. Down there I taught dancing to earn some money, and one of the places I taught was in a school in Orlando run by the father of Vilma and Buddy Ebsen."

Our Judy.

She learned quickly that she didn't have to go through all *that* to make 'em laugh. As Judy told one reporter, "When I found that audiences laughed when I made faces, I figured it was a lot simpler to twitch an eyebrow than to throw myself all out of joint."

However, she wasn't earning all that much from the talent shows, so she had to make a deal with Mama. She had one year to make good, or give up all the showbiz nonsense.

Teaming up with the siblings seemed the smart way of increasing her chances for success, and instantly put more variety into the act.

Left: The dapper Leon. Right: Not quite dapper.

Leon "Zeke" Canova was born on December 31, 1898, and was the first of the Canovas to achieve local fame in the papers with his singing and guitar skills. In the early 1920s, he won the senior contest of the State Federation of Music Clubs held in St. Petersburg, Florida. Studying under the head of the vocal department of the Jacksonville College of Music, baritone Leon soon won a scholarship to the Cincinnati Conservatory of Music, and was chosen to sing roles with the Cincinnati Zoo Opera Company. He played Robert, the executioner, in *Tosca*, and Nicola in *Fedora*.

Returning to Jacksonville, he then worked to develop a recital program to be given in the College of Music's recital hall. He also appeared in a local production of *J.A. Coburn's Minstrels* on November 25, 1922.

Julieta states that her Uncle Zeke "dropped out of high school, and was a very sensitive man, but with a wicked eye for the ladies. He was not book smart, but learned quickly and was a wonderful man. So good at heart that everyone took advantage of him. He was probably a throwback to the Minorcan immigrant side of the family as he loved to garden, loved to sing, and loved animals. He absolutely loved sports — as a spec-

If Zeke crashed it, he ain't cryin'. Ocala, Florida, 1937.

tator. I remember when he was in his sixties and seventies he could sit in his room with the radio tuned to a baseball game, the television to a boxing match, and reading a western novel, and tell you at any point what was going on in all of them. He had a beautiful baritone voice and only spoke English, but made up languages (à la Sid Caesar) when the group had their radio show in Jacksonville, and people would call in to hear the Italian/French/Spanish singer.

"He was married at least twice and his last wife suffered a massive heart attack, and was deprived of oxygen and spent her last years in a [convalescent] home. He visited her every day. When she died, he was devastated. When he died, we found his Bible and the dates inside were the date he was given the Bible, the date he and Iva, his last wife, married and the date Iva passed away. Next to that date he wrote: 'Ivy passed. My only love.'"

(In one of Judy's own scrapbooks is a funny, professionally printed "permit," which states, "This is to certify that I, the legally wedded wife of [signature: Leon Canova] do hereby permit my husband to go where he pleases, drink what he pleases and when he pleases, and I furthermore permit him to keep and enjoy the company of any lady or ladies as he sees fit, as I know he is a good judge. I want him to enjoy life in this world, for he will be a long time DEAD. Signed [Leon].")

Julieta describes the other member of what would be the Canova Trio —

Anne Canova.

Anne, born on September 3, 1903 — as "an extremely talented pianist, stubborn, and always thought her wants and needs should be considered before anyone else's. She did all of the arrangements for the trio and when Mom got her radio show on NBC, she did the orchestrations as well. Anne married a man named Howard Hughes — an interior decorator — and my cousin, Juliana, was Juliana Hughes — a very talented pianist like her mother. When Anne divorced Howard she married John Diggs — a bit player who was a friend of my father, Chester Bearse England.

"Anne always wanted to be center stage and exhibited jealousy of Mom's success. As a result, she and Gogga didn't get along. Gogga knew Mom was the gravy train, and Anne wasn't. Anne was the one that got chased out of the house at knife point, and another time Alma (our Mammy) told us that Gogga threatened to hit Anne over the head with a chair. Anne was not the best of folks, but she and Mom were extremely close. My cousin [her daughter] used to say that if a car were careening down the street towards her [Juliana] and my mom, that her mom [Anne] would save Judy first. Probably true. Anne outlived her son-in-law, my mom, and Zekie."

The great Gogga.

Judy and Anne's first radio effort was broadcast from Jacksonville, Florida's WJAX station with an act called "The Happy Girls." Anne and Zeke had also had time in a Cincinnati station while there for school. Later, with Judy, they became the "Georgia Crackers," helped out by big brother Pete who functioned as their manager. As Judy later told the press, hillbillies *aren't* from Florida, "They and Georgians are 'Crackers.' The only real hillbillies are the mountain folk of Tennessee and of North Carolina. But lately that term has been incorrectly used for almost all types of country people, including even Westerners, which is absolutely wrong. And you'd be surprised at how many boys and gals from Brooklyn are passing on the radio as the genuine article."

The showbiz bug having deeply infected her, Judy left school at age 15 and went to New York with Zeke and Anne, claiming she was 16 in order to work there. Ambitious Judy made another deal with her mama — let them try their luck in NYC, and if they didn't make good, she'd come back and she'd go to college when the time came. Zeke sold his large flock of chickens to scrounge up enough ready cash for the trip and to purchase a "drive-and-share car" going to New York. It wasn't a fun trip, but they had just enough money left to rent a two-room suite in a boarding house — if they didn't eat much.

The Canova trio.

They weren't able to afford a rehearsal hall and were forbidden music privileges in their room, so they took to Central Park for their rehearsals. Seeking out a secluded spot each day, Zeke used a ukulele for accompaniment.

Though hard to believe, it was often written in the press that the trio had never performed a hillbilly song in their lives prior to their New York visit, always performing popular and classical numbers instead. That all changed in New York the day they ran into a guitar-playing friend on the street who advised them that if they could sing hillbilly songs, they could get work in the Village Barn, a new rural nightclub that was just opening. The aspiring musicians immediately went out and bought a book of hillbilly songs, learned several for the audition, and were signed on the spot.

Judy recalled, "We didn't have a skit, music, costumes, or anything. But we started scouting around. Anne and I got together some peasant costumes we thought might be good for a laugh. Our dire necessity drove us to get results. We cooked up a hillbilly skit, and it turned out to be just what the nightclub's patrons wanted. We went in for two weeks, but stayed for twenty-two. Engagements kept piling up and we found ourselves in demand. We were on our way."

They were indeed. At the same time as the Barn, in January of 1931, the trio performed at the Village Nut Club, both gigs for $50 a week. They were a real sensation to the sophisticated city folks.

Whatever the true origin of their hillbilly ways (off the cuff, North Carolina influence, or feeding a nightclub's need), Judy and kinfolk dove into their cornpone characters with total conviction on and offstage.

"Real hillbilly humor," Judy said in 1949, "is dry and earthy and closely bound to folk customs. As for the true hillbilly songs, many of them are Elizabethan, brought over here by the pioneers from England and Scot-

Playing the Palace Theatre in Chicago.

land." She considered "Wabash Cannon Ball" to be the greatest hillbilly song ever written.

At the time of their engagement at the Barn, Judy wrote in John Skinner's newspaper column:

> Dere Mr. Skinner,
>   I am riten' you agin to tell you if you want to here me any more down here at the Village Barn you better hurry because the man that pays me says I have him singin' the same song fer 3 weaks an I tol him that my granpappy singed them 20 years an nobody never said nothing bout it an if they was good enuf fer him to sing that long they was good here fer at least anuther five or six weeks.

I ain't been feelin' so perky — in fact this here New York is gettin' me to feel puniful these las' few weaks so I had to go the doctor an he ast me what I'd bin eatin' an' I tol' him I never et over 20 buckwheat cakes for my mornin' grub — Corse I reckin' that they ain't nobody else that eats catch up and meyernase together like me but they have so many good things to eat here — Anyways te docter said I'd have to quit eaten catchup an' meyernaise toogether or I wouldn' be abel to yodel no more so I gess I will have to quit eaten so much. I don't eat but sevin or ate cakes now, an' I can already tell the diffrince.

Yours trule,
JUDY

Judy, the pigtail princess, now began to adopt the style for which she would become famous: red flannel unmentionables, plaid ginghams, a dowdy straw hat or cowgirl hat just a little too small for the hair parted in the middle, and topped off with cutely beribboned pigtails. (In the late 1940s, it was rumored that those pigtails were insured for $50,000.) And the more Zeke, Anne, and young Judy performed, the more obvious it was who the star was.

CHAPTER TWO
The Tractor to Success

Vaudeville scouts saw the incredible New York Canovas and signed them for a coast-to-coast tour which lasted for over a year beginning in May of 1931. They worked with Bob Albright's act in Oklahoma for a while before hooking up with an RKO unit to the west coast. One newspaper reporter wrote that "during the course of touring they often met a ventriloquist named Edgar Bergen, who used to have his dummy, Charlie

Left: Judy and Harry Langdon. Right: A Zeke on the street.

McCarthy, imitate Judy's hillbilly songs. They thought a man who traveled with a dummy all the time probably got lonesome, so the Canova family invited him to dinner quite often." It would lead to a good running gag "engagement" on Bergen's radio show years later.

The trio received raves during the tour, one newspaper stating that "although Mlle. Ann Codee is the official headliner of the vaudeville array in the RKO Rivoli this week, it is a trio of hill-billy entertainers known simply by their first names of Annie, Judy and Zeke which pilfer the stellar honors right away from her.

"This is no easy task, for the French comedienne has no mean turn herself. But the quaint hill-billy singing of the trio, the piano wizardry of Annie, and the grand clowning of Judy combine to cause what theatrical men style a 'show stop.' In other words, their efforts create such an applause riot that they have difficulty leaving the stage and thus stop the action of the program. They did three encores at the performance we witnessed and even then the cash customers wanted more."

Another review of the same show, on a different night, stated that "their droll, rural comedy antics brought continued applause when they appeared Saturday afternoon, doing a little bit of everything, and each little bit in a finished manner. Annie, for instance, proved herself to be a capable pianist and xylophone player, while Judy's voice seemed capable of countless variations and manipulations. The group yodeled, sang 'mountain' songs, and disported themselves in a manner which won instant popularity."

The burgeoning Canovas also appeared as part of the vaudeville act following Edward G. Robinson's 1932 film, *The Hatchet Man*. One reviewer extolled that "The Three Georgia Crackers…has no equal on the vaudeville stage today." They were often applauded by critics for the "close vocal harmony in hillbilly style" from Judy and Zeke and "excellent piano work" from Annie.

Rudy Vallee caught their act and signed at least Judy on for his *Fleischmann's Yeast Hour* in 1933, which most sources credit as being Judy's big radio break. After that, NBC radio signed the trio for six months before songwriter/producer Lew Brown signed them for his *Calling All Stars* show, which starred Gertrude Niesen, Jack Whiting, and Mitzi Mayfair. During that time, the misnamed "Four Canovas" were negotiating with European managers to do a tour of English music halls and European theaters, after *Calling All Stars*. Sometime during the run of *CAS*, it was announced in the press that they had changed their professional name to the "Four Canovas," though with Pete now handling the business affairs and never mentioned publicly in relation to their performances, obviously this never came about.

Of *Calling All Stars*, Brooks Atkinson of the *New York Times* wrote, "Since Judy Canova and a whole flock of Canovas are in the cast, and since the idea [hillbilly sketch in a mountain cabin] is soundly comic, 'Last of the Hill Billies' may be set down as the most diverting incident in Lew Brown's circus."

Another NYC reviewer's take on the fact that the trio was "an aston-ishing hit" was because "you wouldn't expect 14th Street to enter with such a degree of warmth into the spirit of a hillbilly turn like this, but they did, probably getting a kick out of the exaggerations of rube awkwardness the act uses by way of comedy."

Yet another paper praised, "This Saturday matinee audience turned

somersaults in their seats over the hilarious 'Last of the Hill Billies' skit." It was a routine in which a cabin full of mountain hillbillies is taking pot shots at theatrical agents bent on kidnapping the last of their scruffy coun-try musicians for work on radio and stage. Another amusing number in the show was Lou Holtz and Phil Baker singing a quick mountain ballad at Judy, "We'll run a foot-race to see who wins. Oh, we'll run a foot-race to see who wins. And the one who loses gets you." One December 22, 1934 review stated that the sketches lacked originality and the material was generally "stodgy and uninspired," but called Judy "the applause hit of the show. Doing her own inimitable gargling of one reprise, and later appearing for

an amusing session with Messrs. Baker and Holtz, she panics the customers, ringing down in the finale a hand that tied the show into knots."

But even with all the *good* press, the show closed with a loss of $150,000 after four weeks. As the revue was in a Warner Bros. theater on Broadway, two of the cast members — Judy and Everett Marshall — were salvaged for WB film contracts.

The Canovas didn't have to worry, as there was no shortage of theaters wanting them. When they appeared in vaudeville's Golden Gate Theatre, a reviewer stated, "Everything goes rustic and even the curtain is good, old-fashioned red-and-white-checked calico when Annie, Judy and Zeke, famed 'Three Georgia Crackers,' take the stage. Mountain ballads and dances are the forte of these three from radioland. They haven't been

Playing Loew's Theatre in Atlanta.

long in the city, judging from Zeke's overalls, and the uncreased freshness of Judy's hair ribbon. A mite embarrassed too, by all the applause — or maybe they're just pretending, like."

During the stage tour, the troupe managed to find the time to infiltrate that other popular medium: radio. Already under a six-month contract, the Canova clan proved that a hit is a hit no matter how it's leveled at the masses.

One review of a Wednesday evening performance of theirs on WJZ (NBC) read: "These two girls and a boy have something different on the ball as to hillbilly acts. They utilize the usual accompaniments, such as jug, jew's-harp, piano, violin, guitar, etc., all according to the number being done. Opening with the theme song is an imitation of a whip-poorwill, their song being 'When the Sun Goes Down.' Announcer mentions that the trio [is] from the foothills of the South with authentic songs and style of rendition. Selections offered included 'My Little Home in Tennessee,' by the trio; 'The Mocking Bird' by the boy, who did some bird calls with the aid of the violin, while piano accompaniment was heard in the background; 'In the Valley of the Moon' which is being adopted by the hillbillies as their own; 'Old Model T and Big Rock Candy Mountain.'

"Outstanding feature of the trio appears to be the excellent and natural style of the continuity, plus the nasal twang and comedy lines done by one of the girls [Judy]. The continuity allows for much byplay in the talk anent the various numbers, while in one spot the gal started to tell about the stranger who came to the doorstep wanting to take her photograph. Later on it develops that while she had him covered with the shotgun, the stranger explained that he only wanted to take her picture, which was different and understandable to her. While such bits of talk only take a few moments, it helps the program considerably, and with the other talk lifts it out of the usual run of such offerings. There is plenty of life and a certain freshness in the routine…This trio ought to grab something between now and September."

The Canovas went to play the Café de Paris in London in the mid-1930s, in between New York engagements. Taking an ocean liner over with Mama, Judy loved the trip abroad. Once they were in the UK, she stocked up on plenty of antiques and books.

"All the *best* people went to the Café de Paris," Judy stated. "But I found out that noblemen are no different from regular nightclub audiences. They talk all through your act, too. Bluebloods don't impress me a bit. I shushed them all.

"One night I told a loud table to be quiet, and they didn't seem to mind. The manager did. He said there were four princes at that table and I should be ashamed. 'Well,' I said, 'princes should be polite, too!' And they should, even *more* polite!"

Julieta "Tweeny" Canova stated that "Mom had a terrific work ethic and was always prepared, whether [for] screen work, TV, radio, or live performances. She told me a story about when the four siblings moved to New York to try showbiz. They did their act at a place in New York City called the Village Barn (I think one of us still has a table cloth from there somewhere). And she landed a role in something on Broadway, meet-ing other entertainers in the process — people of whom she stood in awe. She met one of the Barrymore men [evidently John], who was in it. She asked him prior to going on stage the first time, 'Mr. Barrymore, are you ever nervous?' Of course this was while her knees were knocking, and he responded, with a little whiff of gin on his breath, 'Hell, child, I'm *always* nervous.'

The Canovas on radio.

"She and our uncles and Aunt Anne met a tenor whose name was Frank Crabtree — he worked with Eddie Cantor, and Frankie was billed as the 'highest tenor on Broadway.' His stage name was Frank Clarke. Frankie became the caretaker at my Aunt Anne's house and lived into his nineties, always unmarried, always polite, and always loved by the family. One night, in the old days, when they were all trying to put together enough coin to eat at the Automat, or find something even cheaper, they walked to where they were supposed to go eat. They passed a store that had gold chargers in the window with the display of a set of china and crystal. My mom said to Frankie, 'Right now I have twenty cents in my pocket, but when we get famous I'm going to buy gold plates!!'

"And she did. I still have the plates that have a two-inch border of gold design on them. She also said she kept rubbing those two dimes together to see if they'd multiply, but they never did."

Judy *was* becoming famous, independent of the group, or at least gaining the most attention. While most press stories of the mid-1930s were covering the Canova trio, most of the information within was giving little Judy the lion's share of the coverage. Occasionally, she was even requested to pen comic essays in New York papers or national magazines.

In one such article, "Laughter Makes You Beautiful," Judy wrote of her early years, and touched upon what had already thickly painted her onstage character: acknowledging herself as the bawdy, cotton-mouthed frump. Yet this is probably the most revealing autobiographical writing Judy ever put to paper.

When I was a kid, I wasn't a happy character. I was shy and self-conscious and frustrated to the danger point. You see, I was a fat tubby and on the homely side, and still I insisted on wearing the fancy, flouncy dresses that made most of the girls my age look so lovely and attractive. The fact is that I made myself look utterly ludicrous. I looked about as broad as I was long, and I only succeeded in incurring the teasing and laughter of the very children I wanted so much to like me.

As a result, I grew morose and unhappy, which in turn accentuated my homeliness all the more. I became a terrible problem to my mother. Nothing she could think of helped to bring me out of my sullen introversion. I withdrew from normal childhood.

The only thing that could take my mind off myself and my personal unhappiness was music. Zeke and Anne and I went on the radio for a jewelry company when I was 12. Zeke and Anne were fine musicians, and we were going pretty good. When I sang, I could forget myself — I could forget what the little girl named Judy looked like. But the rest of the time I remained terribly unhappy, resigned to a lifetime of having no fun, of being a sober-faced, unhappy wallflower.

Then, the summer I was 12, something happened to change my whole outlook on life. It could have been that my psychological frustration had something to do with aggravating the illness that struck me. It could be that my resistance was lowered by just "not caring." But whatever it was, it laid me low for quite a spell. When I began to recover, Mother took Zeke, Anne and me to the Carolina hills for the summer, to help me regain my strength.

Anne and Zeke went around having fun as all normal kids do, but I stayed inside the cabin, alone. I didn't have any wish to meet any new children and take their teasing or their rebuffs as I had so often done.

Sober-faced, unhappy, I used to sit by the window, listening to the mournfully amusing sound of singing nearby. The native hill people had their own songs, and gradually they began to worm their way into my heart.

And all of a sudden, I, who had forgotten how to laugh, found myself chuckling at the nasal twang of the voices, the funny words, the odd pronunciations — the song lore of the hillbilly!

It was in one of these unguarded moments of laughter that I heard my mother beside me.

"Why, Judy!" she exclaimed joyously, looking down at me. "Judy — you're laughing!" She hesitated as she watched me, and then added gently, "Why, darling — laughter makes you positively beautiful!"

I looked up at her suddenly hurt, disbelieving. *Beautiful? Me?* She was making fun of me! Even though my illness had helped me to lose most of the baby fat which had plagued me so, I was conditioned to considering myself terribly homely. She saw the feeling of disbelief in my eyes, then. She said: "No — don't doubt me, Judy! Come and see for yourself." She took my hand and led me over to the mirror.

Looking at myself, sullen-faced, I thought I was homelier than ever. My face looked a mile long since my illness. My high cheekbones stood out prominently. Despairingly, I looked up at my mother. She said: "Smile, Judy! Go on and smile, and see!"

I made myself smile, a half-hearted smile at first. A diffident smile that contrasted with my usual sullen expression. And swiftly I saw what she meant. Turning the corners of my mouth up *did* do something for me! My face didn't look so long when I smiled. My cheekbones didn't seem nearly so high as they did when the corners of my mouth were drawn down by a scowl. It gave me a new quality — comeliness,

The beautiful one.

radiance, call it what you will. But as I watched my new reflection, I grew happy inside thinking of Mother's words, knowing they were so.

She put a hand under my chin, tilted my face up. "That's a good thing to remember, Judy. Laughter can make anyone beautiful. Give laughter to the world, and you give beauty!"

That advice caught on the top of my heart and hung there. I resolved from that moment to always keep my face alive with a laugh. Curving the lips up had a way of lifting the heart as well. At first it was only on the exterior that I had conquered my unhappy self-consciousness.

Laughter wasn't too easy a habit to form. When Zeke and Anne and I first started our "slap-happy" routines before the public, I was still struggling to treat myself with the therapy of laughter. People would say to my brother, Zeke: "Oh, that sister of yours! She's a card! Doesn't she keep you laughing all day?"

And Zeke would say: "Heck, no — *I* have to make *her* laugh. She's the moodiest gal in town!" But gradually it became second nature — that will to laugh.

And as suddenly as a smile was born within me, a dream came, too. If these songs could work a miracle for me, could bring the magic of laughter to me who had known so little — why couldn't they make other people laugh, too? I had a sudden wish to share this magic. I wanted to bring it to other people who might hide mental depression or physical pain behind a shield of laughter.

In our weeks there in those Carolina hills, I had committed to memory every song I heard, every nasal twang, every oddity of pronunciation. I told Anne and Zeke of my idea to do a routine with much of this hillbilly folk music in it, and they liked the idea.

Three years later, when at 15 I went with Anne and Zeke (and very little capital) to New York with our first "mountain music" routines, there was little about me reminiscent of the morose little sick girl who sat inside that mountain cabin learning the lesson of laughter. The three of us were "rarin'" to go!

The only trouble was, there was little sale for our kind of stuff. We arrived hellbent for Broadway, but That Street was singularly unimpressed. So there were other spots beside

Broadway where people needed to laugh. We pulled a job at the Village Barn out of the proverbial magician's hat. It wasn't much, but it was a job. It paid off in the kind of folding money that bought beans and soothed landlords.

Down in Greenwich Village it was, and here was our opportunity to pull out the stops and let 'er go! We tossed the wacky hillbilly stuff across the footlights and the audience loved it, and we were on our way. The honest laughter of those nightly packed houses paid off.

I laughed and the world began to laugh with me! And as I saw the rooms full of people with their faces transformed by that magic of laughter, I learned true happiness, mental peace, and satisfaction. I was seeing my dream come true — the dream of making people happy. And I knew I had overcome the very drawbacks that had been so great a factor in building my career and my philosophy of life. The advice of my mother — that chance remark — had brought me this happiness, and the fulfillment of this dream:

"Give laughter to the world and you give beauty! Laughter can make you beautiful!"

CHAPTER THREE
Hollywood Found

The Canova group's stage presence had impressed film scouts enough to send for them for a Hollywood try-out. They had a bit part — well, the better part of a song — in Warner Bros.' *Broadway Gondolier* (1935) starring Dick Powell as a cab driver who desperately wants to be an opera singer. The Canovas appear near the beginning of the film during "The Flagenheim Cheese Hour," making sponsor Mrs. Flagenheim (Louise Fazenda) wiggle to the guitar/piano beat against her better judgment. The comedy was released on July 27, 1935.

The trio was back for *In Caliente*, filmed for First National Productions (Warner Bros.) from December 1934 through March 1935 and released on May 25th of that year. Perhaps the funniest bit was Judy's solo song in which she almost ruins "The Lady in Red" number, and gives Edward Everett Horton one of the best shocked "takes" of his career, when she sings her particular loudmouth brand of country into the song as Ed never expected.

Warner Bros.' *Going Highbrow* (1935) was based on a Ralph Spence story entitled "Social Pirates." It was a delightful romantic comedy in the Cinderella vein that gave Edward Everett Horton even more of a chance to do the frantic comedy he did best. It didn't give Judy (minus her siblings) much to do in this slight non-singing role, but it was a start.

She's Annie, best friend and co-worker to Sandy (June Martel) who has all her dreams come true when millionaire Matt Upshaw (Guy Kibbee) plucks her out of the diner she's working at (across from the Waldorf in NYC where Upshaw is staying) because his wife Cora (ZaSu Pitts) wants a daughter quickly in order to instantly get herself into high society. Augie Witherspoon (Horton) has promised Cora that for $50,000 he'll arrange a coming-out party for their "daughter" with Mrs. Marsh (Nella Walker), one of the Fortune 400 set, so, of course, Cora is beside herself with happiness. All's well until Sandy's mistake of a husband, Sam Long (Gordon Westcott), finally catches up with her, just when she's fallen for a good guy, Harley Marsh (Ross Alexander). Augie ends up saving the day, however, by stealing a letter from Sam from his current wife, proving him a bigamist.

Judy has a few lines in the diner, and though there are two songs in the 67-minute feature, she's not a *singing* waitress.

On October 9, 1935 the three Canovas were back together again in Fort Worth, Texas at a testimonial luncheon honoring Paul Whiteman and his orchestra given by the Chamber of Commerce, which included "45 informal minutes with Paul Whiteman."

The following January, Judy hit Broadway big time by joining Bob Hope, Fanny Brice, Eve Arden, and a host of beauties in *The Ziegfeld Follies of*

1936. It ran for 115 performances, from January 30th through May 9th. She lit up the stage in the sketches "The Gazooka," "Amateur Night," and "The Petrified Elevator." Paul Whiteman saw her again at this time and mentioned to Bert McMurtie of CBS that she'd be good for his show. Judy was immediately cast as a regular on Whiteman's *Musical Varieties* during 1936-37. Though Anne and Zeke played a supper club in Florida while Judy was starring in the *Follies*, at least by July 1936 the three of them were performing *together* sometimes for — "The makers of Woodbury's Germ-free Facial Powder and Woodbury's Facial Soap," Paul Whiteman's sponsors.

It was on the Whiteman show that Judy first claimed Unadilla, Georgia, as her hometown. The notoriety she gave to that small town prompted them to officially recognize her as a citizen in 1938, even printing the official statement in many newspapers of the day.

She later told the press how she happened to pick that town: "One day I was traveling through Georgia when the train stopped at a little town called Unadilla. The name fascinated me — it rolled off the tongue so melodiously. On the platform stood an old man and I got to talking to him. With professional interest I asked, 'What do you do here for entertainment?' He looked at me, shifted the tobacco around in his mouth and drawled, 'Well, we just enjoy ourselves in Unadilla, but when we want to be amused, young lady, we go to a smaller town and show off.'

"That sold me on Unadilla, and later, just for a gag, I told people I was born there. Pretty soon, writers began making Unadilla my home town, and letters arrived from Unadilla folks who said they remembered knowing me as a child. Ever since, I've been cured of gags like that."

When the Canova clan first got to Hollywood, they all rented separate living quarters; Judy shared an apartment with her mom, Anne and Pete each had their own place, and Pete lived with his wife. Judy stated at the time, "We live separately because we like to do different things. I don't go around much, partly because I don't know many people here. Some of my Hollywood friends criticize me. They think I'm an old mudstickie because I don't go around a lot just to be seen. I can't figure any connection between being gawked at in the Trocadero and doing a job of acting in a picture.

Takin' 'em by storm!

But Hollywood is like that. Sometimes I get awfully tired of people. Do you ever have an impulse to go off and find a clean place to die?"

By the mid-1930s Judy and her mother were living in a small San Fernando Valley house just a few blocks from the Republic studios. Unfortunately for Anne and Zeke, Hollywood was still only crying out for Judy.

As Julieta states, "Hollywood called and the whole family packed up and came West to make pictures. Except Anne didn't photograph well, and besides, she got preggers [pregnant]. And Zekie didn't like getting up early and learning lines — and wasn't that good of an actor because he was too honest. By this time, Gogga was fed up with Pete, and Mom had that voice, as well as timing."

Still, Anne had her music. At the time, she told the press, "I studied piano for years, and got to the point where I really could play, compose and make my own arrangements, and now [1937] I'm playing *oom-pah* accompaniments!" With the trio now breaking up, Anne appeared on her own in *Adios, Amigo*, a musical revue in Havana, Cuba, and in *Rhapsody U.S.A.*, a musical comedy which toured the South. During the war, Anne regularly entertained troops with her piano boogie-woogie and other musical routines.

Judy and Anne had been writing some songs together all the while, a few of which were collected in *Popular Mountain Songs* (1934), a songbook sporting one of several different covers, proving that Hollywood wasn't always trying to deglamourize Judy Canova.

Hannah My Love
(Music by Anna Canova, Lyrics by Judy Canova)

Oh Hannah my love come give me
Your hand in mine to hold
And tell me I'm the man you'll marry
Don't treat me mean and cold

I ride to church on Sunday
My true love passed me by
I knowed her mind was a changin'
By the movements in her eyes

When her parents saw me coming
They flew into a rage
"You must not steal my daughter
For she is under age."

I'd sail all over the ocean
I'd sail all over the deep
I think of lovin' Hannah
And then lay down and sleep

Kind sir, to steal your daughter
I never yet did try
But court her in some bridge room
I never will deny

The original glamour girl.

Whoa Back Buck
(Music by Anna Canova, Lyrics by Judy Canova)

Made a crop last year with a one-horned ox
This year plowed a mulie
When I gather my cotton and corn
I'm a goin' back to Judy

(chorus:)
Whoa Back Buck says git up, Sam
Step on the cotton like you don't give a D---
Whoa Buck Whoa Buck Whoa Buck whoa
Who made your back band I don't know

Never made no cotton at all this year
Cabbage or tomatoes
Land so poor it wouldn't sprout nothin'
But ole cowpeas and taters

(repeat chorus)

Fellow tied his dog in my backyard
Never said a word about it
I ain't no hand to start a row
But I'm a devil when a row gets started

(repeat chorus)

Made a crop and a half of cotton last year
Hadn't ought to have told it
When I got my taters done
Some sun-of-a-gun done stole it

(repeat chorus)

The Snake-Eyed Killin' Dude
(Music by Anna Canova, Lyrics by Judy Canova)

Old Jud Mason had three sons all killed off in a feud
One was left and they called him The Snake-Eyed Killin' Dude
Leather boots all slick and shined blue shirt and flowin' tie
Trousers neat, belt full of lead, slouch hat down o'er one eye
On a stump just off the road is where he allus shot
With his gun across his knee, when he said stop you'd stop
He was slyer than a fox and quicker than a snake
Ev'ry time he pulled his gun a grave they'd have to make
When they shot him in the back he started in to grin
Told his folks to shine his shoots before they buried him

'Cause I Got the Fever in My Bones
(Music by Anna Canova, Lyrics by Judy Canova)

Oh the sun shines overhead
But I'm laying in my bed
'Cause I got the fever in my bones
I can hear the birds outside
And the bobcats cry all nite
While I got the fever in my bones
While I got the fever in my bones

I can't sleep at all, at all
Ev'rything I eat is gall
'Cause I got the fever in my bones
Takin' quinine bitter root
Till my hide's a heather boot
Still I got the fever in my bones
Still I got the fever in my bones

In the morn my chill comes on
And my mind begins to roam
'Cause I got the fever in my bones
As I lay here day by day
I can't even load my hay
'Cause I got the fever in my bones
'Cause I got the fever in my bones

From the swamp the skeeters fly
See 'em fly and pass me by
'Cause I got the fever in my bones
And I know I'm gittin' worse
Who can make and move a curse?
Good Lord take the fever in my bones
Good Lord take the fever in my bones

The Fatal Shot
(Music by Anna Canova, Words by Judy Canova)

The other day I overheard a story
Worse I've heard in many years
And maybe it was only just a story
Still it filled my eyes with tears

It seems a man who hadn't seen his daughter
Since the day her mother died
The day the poor wife died folks took the baby
And brought it up far from his side

The daughter grew to be a fine young lady
Often asked about her dad
And tho' he sent much money to support her
People told her he was bad

The daughter first believed the people's story
But within her heart somehow
She longed to see the man they called her father
Nothing seemed to matter now

One day she found an address in the bureau
Then she went and packed her bag
She wrote a note and left it in the mailbox
On the train time seemed to lag

She reached a little village in the morning
No one would offer to direct her there
But someone said her Pa lived near the Swamp Road
Take her there he wouldn't dare

She found the place and someone coming t'wards her
Father, that's the only word she said
He didn't hear but said, "You Re-ve-noo-er"
Then he aimed and shot his daughter dead

CHAPTER FOUR
Star and First Wife

By the time Judy Canova had invaded *The Edgar Bergen/Charlie McCarthy Show* in 1937, she was officially a radio draw. She quickly struck up a romantic rapport on the series, playing out a mock romance with the master ventriloquist. The relationship gag lasted a good while, with ample publicity choked out of it. When she "broke up" with Bergen in September of 1937 (because of Charlie McCarthy, of course), Judy told

Radio's true romance: Judy and the dummy.

the press: "We had a quarrel Sunday and now it's all over. I've heard nothing but Charlie this and Charlie that. The dummy has become an obsession with Eddie. Now he can have his Charlie. I don't want to play second fiddle to a dummy." She returned in the fall of 1938 for Bergen's *Chase and Sanborn Hour*.

Film work continued to be just as plentiful. Paramount's *Artists and Models* (1937), based on a series of New York revues 10 years earlier, put Judy in the role of Toots, roommate to beautiful, ambitious Paula Sewell (Ida Lupino) who's eager to be the Queen of the Artists and Models ball, because it looks like the winner of that is also going to be "the Townsend Girl," the model for Townsend Silver's million dollar ad campaign. Mac Brewster (Jack Benny), head of the Brewster Advertising Agency and Paula's unofficial boyfriend, touts her for the position, but Alan Townsend (Richard Arlen) doesn't want a model; he wants a beautiful socialite. The only thing Paula can do is go with Toots to Miami, where Alan is spending some time so she can let herself be discovered by Alan's set. The plan works perfectly, but she didn't expect to fall for the guy. When Mac appears, he doesn't spill the beans; he just wants what's best for her. The beans spill anyway when Alan's mother finds some professional ads that Paula posed for. Alan is upset but gives her the Townsend Girl account anyway — but

Funnin' for the camera with the Yacht Club Boys.

that's all. Paula is heartbroken, even though she has just what she's always wanted: fame. Mac starts seeing Cynthia Wentworth (Gail Patrick), so he's alright. When Toots straightens Alan out that Paula's been heartsick since they broke up, Paula gets her guy and she's alright, too.

Along the way there's songs and comedy a-plenty, the best being from the antics of Judy and her rubbery lover (Ben Blue), a rainmaker (yep, he

The most elastic scene in film history. Artists and Models, *1937.*

can do it) and giddy & flexible dancer. Judy's first appearance is a bubbly bathtub number called "Pop Goes the Bubble," hardly racy with that one-piece swimsuit she's wearing in the tub. She and Anne and Zeke also have an immobile comedy number at the ball near the picture's end, with Judy doing about the only movement in the piece; Anne just sits and stares and sings like a zombie while Zeke is plum happy just to lean on the bar

The three Canovas in Thrill of a Lifetime, *1937.*

and belt out his song. It was a good picture for Judy. No wonder she got double billing — as herself in the regular cast, and along with Anne and Zeke further down in the credits.

Daughter Diana says, "I saw a very early bit of her in *Artists and Models* with Ben Blue. She was very young and she did this duet with him where her physical comedy was unbelievable. She was extremely flexible when she was a kid. So much so that when the circus came to town one year they must have seen her on the beach and asked her if she wanted to join them! Anyway, in this film she used that rubber-band ability along with her voice. Nobody had ever seen that before."

The 75-minute Paramount picture *Thrill of a Lifetime* (1937) put The Yacht Club Boys, a four-guy singing group (Jimmy Kern, Charlie Adler, George Kelley, Billy Mann) with the same manic energy as the Ritz

Brothers, in the spotlight while young Judy and Ben Blue again provide the main romantic comedy.

Stanley (Johnny Downs), Betty Jane (Eleanore Whitney), and Judy are sent for by producer Sam Wattle (Franklin Pangborn) to offer them a job in his new show — but only if they drop Judy. That's fine by Stanley who considers Betty Jane's sister more of a third wheel on their act,

Thrill of a Lifetime, *1937*.

but his sweetheart refuses to perform without her sister. The solution to the problem is a visit to Camp Romance, an island resort-camp where people come to fall in love. Howard "Howdy" Nelson (Leif Erickson) runs the place, believing that love is a scientific thing; that's why he's written a play, *There Ain't No Such Thing As Love*, which he wants Mr. Wattle to produce. The three down-on-their-luck performers pool their financial resources for a five-day stay so that Judy, unbeknownst to her, can find her man, thereby finally making their act a twosome.

They are joined in the camp by the harmonizing Yacht Club Boys who pretend to be the Wattle Brothers, but this crazy foursome would rather eat ravenously, meet girls, and duck the issue of the play. When cornered by Nelson, they say a tryout here in the camp would be a grand idea before springing it on Broadway, and that's just what everyone starts planning.

Meantime, Judy has already fallen for Skipper (Ben Blue), the rather timid captain of the boat that brought them to the island. Though Stanley keeps trying to set Judy up with the lifeguard, Don (Larry "Buster" Crabbe), she keeps finding Skipper, and what a happy couple they make.

When the real Mr. Wattle arrives, the YC Boys call him crazy and convince Nelson to lock him up so the show (and their free vacation) can go

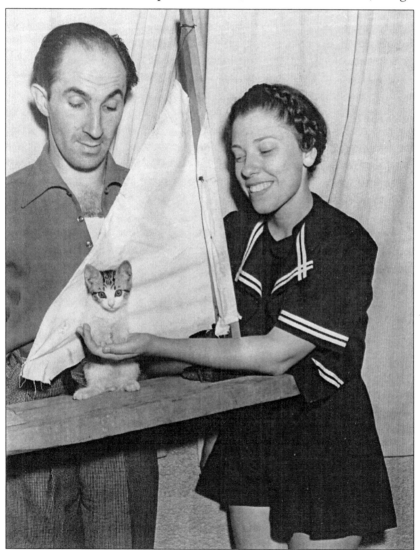

Ben Blue and Judy.

on without a hitch. Luckily Judy happens on a telegram which tells the truth and springs Wattle from his prison cabin just in time for him to catch most of the show, which he, of course, loves and wants to produce on Broadway, with everyone reprising their roles.

A lot happens in a little time, and there's much to commend about this little film. In one scene, Judy sings that it's "Sweetheart Time" to her little boy Blue, making them both fall asleep into a wacky dream ballet in which the happy couple toss big balloons at one another. When Judy trespasses on the camp's hick next-door neighbors, it's a great opportunity to take out the git-tar and twang "You're Nobody's Daughter" with Zeke and Anne. The three of them harmonize a delightful little number, ending in another impressive Judy yodel, of course. Perhaps the funniest thing about the film is that putting on Nelson's *play* has no dialogue or plot; it's merely a revue with songs. Still, it gives Betty Grable (playing Nelson's lovesick secretary) a chance to show off her tap dancing and Ben Blue to slide around the stage in a wordless "skating" number. Not to mention putting the Three Canovas on stage again for another brief guitar and harmony warble.

The family was close, keeping in constant touch whenever they moved out of each other's immediate circle for even a short time. In early 1939, business manager Pete wrote:

> Dear Dude Anne & Zeke:
> I took the liberty of coming up this morning to send Judy's furs to open her letter to Mama as I thought there may be something important. The reason you have not heard [from me] is that we have all been sick at the beach. I started on medicine Monday and just yesterday had to come up to the dentist and come back again today.
> Mama went down on Saturday and spent Saturday and Sunday with Annie Meroni and we went down Sunday night and took her to the cottage. She went to bed Sunday night and has not been out of bed since. Me and Florence have been nursing her, she got a terrible head cold and has been running fever up to 102, but the fever broke yesterday and she is much better. Says she could get up today, but we are making her stay in bed and will let her get up tomorrow. So much for that. We didn't want to worry you all and she didn't want me to write about it until she was better, so now I don't think there is anything to worry about.

Judy, I put the money of the check into your account, so if you are broke you can draw a check in the name of Judy Canova on the Barnett Bank. I haven't had time to figure up the money and will take it all to the beach this afternoon and forward checks to Anne and Zeke and your balance to New York. I will also draw a check on the [Social] Security for three thousand dollars by Mama and deposit it to your Jacksonville account before the week is over, so you will be fully protected. ...

I am feeling a little better and would like for you to let me know when rehearsal will start for the show. Hope you will have a good time while you have the week off. Don't step too high, but give old Harry a whirl around the ring again.

In March of 1939 he wrote again:

Dear Anne:

I am very sorry I was not able to write you more explicitly concerning the Atlanta engagement. We are in there on a salary and a percentage and the reason I wrote you to come immediately is that I am not well, however, I wanted to have Connie drive me to Atlanta and to help me distribute window cards, etc. in order to try and beat the percentage figure.

Judy told me to wire you over her name to come immediately as she wanted the three of you to learn Hold Tight, a good swing number, however your wire and letter state you are not coming, so there is nothing more I can do about it. Suppose the publicity thing will just have to go and we will do just the business we can. However, inasmuch as you had to come, I certainly thought you would pay more attention to business than stayin' out there where you are not earning one dime. However, Sugar, that is your business and no concern of mine.

It would be well for you to write me immediately on receipt of this letter and let me know just exactly what your plans are. If you are going straight to Atlanta, naturally rehearsals are out.

Judy will go to Jena tomorrow and I will stay quiet and try and get better. Am trying hard to line up some dates after Atlanta, but they don't want to pay us anything and I feel we would be very foolish to kick under about salary as the show might not turn out the way we expect.

There is no more news. Please write so I will know exactly what you are going to do.

Love,
Pete

Now that her career was going places, with more confidence and beaus coming out of the woodwork, Judy had a chance at a proper social life.*

She first met Chester B. England in London in 1939 while she was on a vaudeville tour, and he was a student at Cambridge. According to an interview given to Joseph Kaye, Judy met Chet in the London nightclub where she was performing. "Chet was visiting England with his family," she recalled. "I was homesick and wishing hard to see an American face, when someone brought Chet backstage to meet me. I gave him such an enthusiastic 'Glad to meet you,' that he may have had the idea this was some strange case of love at first sight. Maybe it was. Anyway, it was a delightful meeting. But it was four years before I saw him again."

In the meantime, Judy fell for another soldier. How she met and why she married James H. Ripley is still uncertain, but it was a quickie marriage that didn't last long.

And on October 8, 1941 Judy went into court all in black — dress, hat, shoes, stockings, purse — to receive her annulment from Cpl. Ripley. She wept as she told the tale of their whirlwind courtship — they were engaged on June 10th and married four days later in Hawaii. As she told one reporter, "It was that beautiful, soft moon. It sort of reached down and put its arm around my shoulder. There was a nightingale on a telegraph post, and I just got swept over by love." She didn't know he was in the service, as he failed to stipulate that on the marriage license application. She discovered he was an AWOL Army officer (a corporal) after arriving at their bridal suite, when soldiers came in to remove him to Fort Ruger. Judy told the court that when they took him out "he said he was doing accounting for the government; that he had been sent to Hawaii on a difficult matter, a sort of secret service matter for the government." She sought the annulment because she couldn't trust him anymore. "He deceived me and told me lies; his being a soldier didn't have anything to do with it."

---

*Judy is rumored to have been secretly married to comedian Bob "Bazooka" Burns in 1936, but there is no evidence to support that claim.

Ripley didn't appear in court, at which point Judy swore an affidavit that he was no longer in the military. She thought he might be back home in Montgomery, Alabama. She later despondently told the press, "I wonder why people think marriage and divorces are expected in Hollywood? They happen everywhere. My goodness, from all the hullabaloo raised about what happened in Honolulu, you'd think I was an important person. Just because I live in Hollywood…"

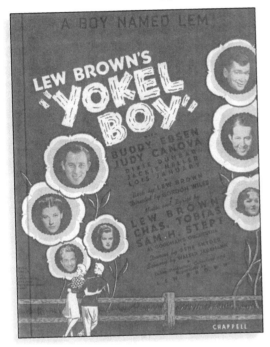

After Ripley, Judy was seen in the company of Hollywood attorney Warren McKinney, going "steady" since the annulment, but that didn't last either.

If romance wasn't her true calling, at least work was lucrative. Around this time she was earning about $1,700 a week from radio and $4,300 a week from pictures. Not to mention knocking 'em dead in her newest Broadway show, *Yokel Boy*.

As Judy's official bio stated at the time, "she was again contacted by Lew Brown to star in his show then in production called *Yokel Boy*. Judy had never deviated from her hillbilly characterizations up until *Yokel Boy*, at which time Mr. Brown called on her to carry the burden of putting the song numbers used over to the public. Judy introduced the popular 'Comes Love' number from the show, and was seen in three or four characterizations, her favorite of which was 'Catherine the Great,' her next, 'Time for Jookin', and 'Lem and Sue.' Judy lived up to Mr. Brown's expectations and was the hit of this show as attested to by the hardboiled New York dramatic critics. She was acclaimed by several as America's Bea Lillie and by others as having one of the most natural coloratura voices seen on the New York stage. She has recently been signed by Republic Pictures for a series of pictures, the first of which will appear soon, entitled *Scatterbrain*, and here is one little lady that has proven the old adage: 'Thar's gold in them thar Hillbilly Songs.'"

Gold there was. A friend of the family, Jesse Kaye, who had Lew Brown's ear, wrote to Pete, who was then in Jacksonville, Florida on June 20, 1939, of the status of the show:

Dear Pete,

I was in Boston yesterday at the opening of the show.

To sum the whole thing up quickly, Pete, there is no question but that Judy was the hit of the show so far as her songs were concerned. She stopped them cold in a couple of places. Naturally, she has more lines to do than when you were first on the grounds for rehearsal, but not nearly what she is entitled to. She is one of the few people who does her lines very well and just as we discussed when you were here, I am confident that Brown is now going to work and tie Judy in much closer.

At the finish of the show in the Trocadero scene, Anne, Judy and Zeke step out for a specialty and they did "Ole Man Mose" and stopped the show — at 12 o'clock; and then they did "St. Louise Blues," as an encore. Everybody, naturally, was happy about this fact but everyone felt it was not right to have those two alien tunes in there. Judy told Brown it would be all right with her to take them out if he will write something for them which she has been trying to get him to do for some time.

Pearl, at the present time, is not good in the show. He seems to be the only weak point and he is an important cog which makes it very pressing for Lew to either whip him into shape or get rid of him.

Lew talked to me at great length about Judy, cutting her salary for the first two weeks. How unfair it was that she wouldn't do it and that she was the only one and that he wanted me to get in touch with you and make you see the light. He is very tenacious about this; evidently more from the principle than the actual money he would be saving, although every dollar he can save will help him on this break-in date. He talked to me along the following lines: "You know I like Judy and I would not do anything to hurt her and give them [songs] to others in the show, etc., etc., etc." You know, Pete, that a man in Brown's position can be vindictive if he wants to, and hurtful. As far as Judy is concerned, however, she is very necessary to his show and I don't know how or why any

man in his right senses would do anything to hurt the real
star of the show, but rather break his neck to push her along;
but Brown is not the average business man and sometimes
does a lot of ridiculous things that cost him eventually a lot
of money because of some action that gripes him, such as
Judy not taking a cut.

I am giving you the details, Pete, because you are not
here and I think you should know what's going on and how
Brown's mind is functioning. He has been very nice to all
of us and I would not like to see him change his attitude.
Frankly, Pete, I don't know what to advise. If Brown were
the average, normal person, I would say definitely "do not
cut because he would not dare to jeopardize his production
by hurting his star," but you know Lew, maybe better than I
do and I would like you to weigh this point.

I am enclosing herein one of the notices. They are all practically the same. I think the newspapers were kinder to the
show than they were entitled to be; however, that's Brown's
good fortune.

I am also enclosing copy of the Program.

Best regards,
Sincerely,
Jesse Kaye

P.S. Regarding Judy's billing, we have been studying this;
that is, Judy, Mr. Partington, Sam Rauch and a few other boys
who are not prejudiced and we feel that the billing as it is
with Judy on the end, is more eye-catching than if she were
in the center. It seems to us that the two names that stood out
on the boards and newspaper advertisements, etc. were Pearl
and Canova. We definitely feel, Pete, this is not a point to
get into any serious discussion with Brown about but rather
to hold this back of our mind to throw up to Brown at some
later date, if necessary. What do you think?

On June 26th Kaye wrote to Pete again that things were quieter
between Brown and Canova on the money side, but artistic differences
still reigned. Anne was not happy with the song they wrote around "Ole
Man Mose Is Dead." Kaye told Anne "to ask Judy to learn it as well as
she could and at least try it at one show, if Brown demanded it, and prove

to him that it was no good. In this way he could never say that she did not follow his instructions and did not even attempt to give the song a chance.

"Another thing, Pete, we are in a very peculiar business and it's awfully hard to tell whether a song is good or bad. Even 'Ole Man Mose' was around for a long time before it became popular."

Herbert Drake's review of *Yokel Boy* in the *Boston Herald* was mixed, calling it a show with "several really good songs, and a handsome cast, but it is not quite enough to be more than a fairly amusing evening." However, Judy was singled out as "a mountain gal comedian with a loosely articulated skeleton and jagged vocal chords. She sings 'Comes Love' with devastating effect and carries on with gamboling abandon, but falls off the crags when she tries an item about Catherine the Great. That one requires a mountain cabin Bea Lillie."

Most reviews were mostly directed at producer/writer/director Lew Brown, one stating that "the composers and lyricists probably remain the stars. In order: Mr. Brown, Charlie Tobias and Sam H. Stept. If they just had a book, too, theirs would be something beyond a summer show." But again, "up there on the stage is Judy Canova of the Ann, Zeke and Judy Canovas. A rowdy mixture of Beatrice Lillie and other comediennes along parallel lines in the general direction of Fanny Brice, this one pretty much puts the summer in its place. As 'Catherine the Great' she tells the legend of that lady of the Russians, in 'Junkin" she interprets the South, with 'Comes Love' she shows that she can look at an honest sentiment, face to face. Quite a girl, on the whole."

Another review stated that "her song at the piano with Ann and Zeke Canova stopped the show." The *New York Telegram* was also very positive: "There are so many superb things about Lew Brown's *Yokel Boy*. Admitting its faults — and it has plenty of them, including a wispy book that might be thrown away without any definite damage — it still brims with talent, sparkling music and the best ensemble dancing you ever saw outside of Rockefeller Center. Miss Canova's style of comedy is exactly what you would expect after hearing her on the radio, but you may be surprised at her agility and stage presence."

The show, which also starred Buddy Ebsen, ran for 208 performances from July 6, 1939 until January 6, 1940.

When Republic Pictures bought the rights and finally made a film of the same name in 1942, not only did they *not* use the plot or characters of the stage piece, they didn't even put Judy in the film, though she was under contract to them. They *did* use Judy's regular co-star, Eddie Foy, Jr., but it was Joan Davis, for some reason (who took over for Betty Keane, after she severely sprained her ankle at the beginning of the film's shooting) who became the star. The film did, however, contain two of the show's original songs: "It's Me Again" and "Comes Love."

Judy thought that the Republic contract was what really broke up the trio. "I was so sorry about that because Anne, Zeke and I had had so much fun together. My brother Pete had been with us, too, as business

"To my Foncie & Pete — the bestest 'sister' and brother ever — you're always in my heart. Love, Judy."

manager. But you can't write movies to star three people — look at the Ritz Brothers. So I had to take the contract and split up the trio — and they all have more talent than I!"

It didn't take long for Zeke to feel the financial squeeze. He wrote to Judy at the end of March 1940:

> Dearest Honey,
>
>   Well I'm some tired tonite. I thought sure we would be finished by this time and it's costing me more than I thought. But maybe I can sell the place when I get it fixed up. Two places sold around here in the last three weeks.
>
>   Hilda & John drove by here yesterday and wanted me to go home with them and fish some. You would be crazy about him. That's really something when a person is dying and they want to hear us B.Cast [broadcast] before they die. Everybody wants to see us back on the air. You couldn't pull 10 weeks out of the bag could you? Just got a letter from Ann and I'm sorry I missed your egg hunt.
>
>   I'm really crazy about the widow and her child. I sure love that kid. So you see, if I got married I'd have my family. The child is only three years old. I gave her the Charley McCarthy and she was tickled to death with him.
>
>   Sure hope mother is feeling good. I sure wish she was down here so we could go fishing. Smoked ham's are selling for ten cents a lb. and bacon ten cents, good thing we didn't go in the hog business and I bought eggs for ten cents a dozen. I got rid of all my chickens, couldn't afford to feed them.
>
>   Well I'm glad you had such a nice rest before your picture and I hope you and the family are feeling good by this time. Sure wish I could see you. It was a beautiful Easter yesterday but today was very cool. Sure enjoyed your letter, write again soon. Tell mother to write.
>
>   Love to all,
>   Zeke.

To be fair, how *could* Judy have passed up a film contract? Especially when the head of the studio was doting on her.

Judy's oldest daughter recalled, "You have to understand, Herb Yates — Herbert J. Yates — who was the head of the studio, had a *huge* crush on

Judy is *hot stuff.*

British music hall, stage and screen actress Gracie Fields with Judy near La Canzione Del Mare, Ms. Fields' home on the Isle of Capri. Judy and Fili visited Ms. Fields when in Europe on their honeymoon.

Mom. Didn't matter whether she was married, divorced, dating, engaged, whatever. He was gaga over her to the point that our grandmother, Grandma Hitler — Retta — absolutely thought he was the most terrible human on the face of the earth. He was easily more in the range of someone who would be a young suitor for Retta than for Mom. He even dyed his hair to look younger. And Mom was a hottie when she was that age. Yates showered her with gifts, favors, and when he finally realized she was going to marry my stepfather — Diana's dad — he decided to marry Vera Ralston instead. When Mom married Fili, Yates made all the arrangements for their European honeymoon. I don't know if he paid for all of it through the studio, but I wouldn't be surprised."

CHAPTER FIVE
Hittin' the Heights

With a new film contract growing ripe, and a slue of strong radio performances behind her, the only thing Judy lacked at the start of the new decade was her *own* radio series. She was looking for the right vehicle — and she let everyone know it.

The family was helping, even with the Trio now well and truly split to the wind. On March 4, 1940, kinswoman H.L. Canova tried her hand with a radio idea for Judy:

FAMILY NIGHT
with
JUDY CANOVA

Family Night is to be a presentation either thirty or sixty minutes weekly of different talented families on the radio. It must be understood in order to compete that at least Father, Mother and Child must compete, i.e., there must be present at least a family consisting of three members. In the event, large families compete at the discretion of the producer.

This is not to be a quiz show, or to be handled in any manner whereby any of the contestants are held up to ridicule for the sake of laughs.

It is tentatively decided that the audience will nominate the winning family by their applause, second, third, and remaining winners also in the same manner. CASH prizes — which will have to be of sufficient amount to insure a ready response from participants — will be awarded to the winners each night.

Miss Judy Canova is to act as Mistress of Ceremonies and the dialogue of Family Night is to be kept at the absolute minimum in order to allow for as much time as possible for the contestants.

Any family regardless of race, creed or color, providing that at least three members appear before the microphone, is eligible. Their talents may be shown in various ways, singing, tap dancing, instrumentations, imitations, recitations, etc.

It is further proposed that each week the listening audience will send in their "Family Pet Peeve," for which, when used on the air, they will also be awarded a Cash prize. It is the intention to use as many peeves each week as there are families participating on the program. A peeve will be read to each family and their reaction to same will be given over the air, at which time the name of the party sending in the

peeve will be announced. All peeves to become the property
of Judy Canova.

It's doubtful that an "absolute minimum" of dialogue would have
excited Judy much. Still, a response to the idea from Pete led to further
explanation from H.L.: "You mentioned in your wire, the lower the figure
[budget], the easier to sell. I can appreciate this, but I feel we should definitely look on this as a good thirty minute show — after all, it has proven
in Bowes' [Amateur Hour] case, why shouldn't it prove for us? — and try
to sell it for the first thirteen weeks for as much as possible. There will
have to be a lot of money spent on this show and naturally I want to get
as much as possible in order to insure getting Judy's services. Incidentally,
as to Judy's work on this record, let me point out when you are in a drab
studio making a record with no audience participation, it is mighty hard
for an artist of her type to get the most out of a script. It is not my intention that this be a script production, but I feel Judy's spontaneity working
only from notes will make a very homey show. If the peeves sent in furnish an opportunity for Judy to get comedy out of them, I don't feel this
angle should be overlooked.

"What will be necessary for the production of this show: two piano
players, production manager, one assistant, one secretary, one writer, trans-
portation, budget for guest artists, weekly prizes for families competing,
peeve prizes, telephone, telegrams, stationery, and stamps. With such an
expense I feel we should endeavor to get five thousand dollars for the
first thirteen weeks."

It just didn't feel right, so Judy passed on the idea. Things were hap-
pening fast in between films, though. On August 27, 1940, her attorney,
Charles H. Kelman, wrote to inform her that a new Ziegfeld show was
being cast, and she was wanted as the lead comedienne: "I believe he will
be inclined to pay about $600 or better per week. The rehearsal will start
in October 1940. Since the Follies were always lucky for you, it might be
wise to give this offer very serious consideration, if same will not conflict
with your present motion picture arrangement. Please discuss this matter
at length with Pete and advise me of your intentions." (Regardless of the
show's promise, it was not to be among Judy's professional credits.)

He also stated, "I finally got around to seeing your picture 'Scatter
Brain' in the RKO Theatre, and must admit that you 'did yourself proud.'
There is a definite improvement in your technique over the last picture."

Scatterbrain (1940) had nothing to do with idiots, unless you count
producer/director J.R. Russell (Alan Mowbray) who is eager as heck to

find a true redneck to star in his new Ozark Mountains picture. At least that's what he tells the press: that he's determined to put realism in Hollywood for a change. But what he *really* wants is a competent actress who can dish out the country twang. Eddie MacIntyre (Eddie Foy, Jr.) thinks he's setting up his girlfriend Esther Harrington (Isabel Jewel) for the role, but J.R. and the press arrive just when it's Judy's turn to pull the plow, and she's discovered by mistake. The rest of the picture is wrapped up in J.R. and Eddie putting their heads together to figure out how to get out of using this hick. It's not until a party is given by the head of Perfection Pictures that they realize this girl's got talent!

Newspaper stories state that *Scatterbrain* cost Republic Pictures a measly $125,000 to make, and by the mid-1940s had already grossed over $600,000. It didn't look like a costly picture, with so many office scenes between the two real stars of the picture, Alan Mowbray and Eddie Foy, Jr. Not many songs either, with the final production number, "Scatterbrain," being the only big one in the show. It *was* a funny picture, though; just not quite enough Judy.

Puddin' Head (1941) has more, and puts Judy — Judy *Goober*, that is — in the driver's seat when the United Broadcasting System accidentally builds their new $3 million building one foot onto her land. Idiot Harold L. Montgomery, Sr. (Raymond Washburn) and his equally doltish son, Junior (Eddie Foy, Jr.), attempt to hookwink Judy, who sings when she's scared, into making her think she's a radio star, but she's really singing into a dead mike. But when Uncle Lem (Slim Summerville) accidentally taps into UBS's cable, Judy is live on the Puddin' Head Baking Powder Show, delighting the sponsors and winning herself a top recording contract.

Sources claim that its $750,000 budget was the largest ever for a Canova film, employing 1,500 extras. Production was halted for a time by Republic when Judy insisted upon director approval and a say in the script and casting. It also looked like Buster Keaton was going to play

Judy's beau for a time, but he apparently never made it into the final shoot, much of which was shot on location in Pasadena, California, in April and May of 1941. A solid score of Jule Styne/Eddie Cherkose songs filled the film, including a musical version of what became one of Judy's most ungrammatical of catchphrases — "You're Telling I."

The Republic flicks were paying off, financially *and* artistically. Iowa

A bone chilling scene from Puddin' Head.

City's *Press-Citizen* stated that *Puddin' Head* "proves again that good, clean fun is the screen's best bet when it comes to entertainment." When the film was re-released in Southern states in 1949, it outgrossed 60% of the new films on the market; especially at the Globe Theatre in New Orleans.

During the filming of *Puddin' Head*, Judy developed a cold which seemed to be a result of having her tonsils out the previous year, and delayed *Scatterbrain's* production somewhat also. Judy told the press, "The studio made me take out my tonsils last year. Before that I'd just been getting sore throats and holding up production. They yanked out the tonsils, and I haven't had any sore throats since. But colds — man, the colds!"

One of Judy's biggest musicals was *Sis Hopkins* (1941), based on the 1899 play by Carroll Fleming and Edward E. Kidder. Republic Pictures bought the film rights for $50,000, putting in a phenomenal $100,000 advertising budget on top of the already $300,000 production costs. The luscious Susan Hayward was borrowed from Paramount, while press reports indicate that Carole Landis and Jane Frazee were both sought for Judy's role. Naturally it wouldn't have been nearly the musical it was had not someone of Judy's singing skill manned the lead. *Lots* of songs dot the 98-minute feature. *Sis Hopkins* also claimed to be the first picture filmed on the former site of Mack Sennett's old studio, where Mabel Normand filmed her comedy hits.

The plot: When rich plumbing tycoon Horace Hopkins (Charles Butterworth) gets his picture in the paper with the mistaken caption that he's out of a job, he receives a kindly invite by mail from his niece, Sis Hopkins (Judy), that he can stay with her for a spell while he gets back on his feet. Horace is a simple working man, though his wife Clara (Katharine Alexander) and pretty daughter Carol (Susan Hayward) are social-climbing snobs who object to the simple country girl coming to live with them. When she doesn't seem to fit in, Horace offers the girl a chance for a college education at Carol's school, and Sis is only too glad to take him up on it. Poor Sis doesn't realize that she's the joke of the campus and an utter disgrace for Carol to bare, the two of them being roommates. Lucky for Sis she's taken under the wing of the Professor (Jerry Colonna). The professor had overheard the girl singing and — impressed by her ability — puts her in his latest show.

Carol is jealous of Sis's talent and her ability to make friends easily, so she tries to get her expelled by planting her on stage in the local burlesque theatre during a raid. But it's not until Horace gets in trouble with one of the fleeing strippers (she climbs into his bedroom with not much on during the raid and he lets her wear Clara's mink coat just to get rid of her) that Sis gets into big trouble (retrieving the coat for him which the girl freely returns). Of course Sis can't tell the Dean the *real* reason she was arrested with the coat, and she decides to return home on the night of the big show. As luck would have it, there's a talent scout in the audience that night who is thinking about taking the whole show to Broadway. So the professor rides his bicycle over to get her off the train and cart her back onto the stage to wow them in the grand finale. And that's just what happens.

Great songs and super support from bug-eyed Jerry Colonna make this one of Judy's best ensemble pictures.

With Colonna's help, *True to the Army* (1942) was possibly Judy's best World War II film, a short-but-sweet 76 minutes with a full kitbag of songs and comedy. Filmed from late October to mid-November, 1941 with the working titles of "Private Yoo Hoo" and "Sergeant Yoo Hoo,"

Army's release was delayed until June 14, 1942 because of the Japanese attack on Pearl Harbor. Most of the songs were penned by Harold Spina and Frank Loesser, with the exception of Judy's version of the classic, "I Can't Give You Anything But Love." But it was the combination of tap dancing Ann Miller and the Canova/Colonna comedy combo that raised this one above the average war fare.

Colonna and Canova, one damn fine comedy team!

The plot: "Broadway Bill" Chandler (Allan Jones) is obsessed with making his morale-boosting show for the Army the best it can be here at Fort Bray, so he's always on the lookout for great talent. Meantime, poor Daisy Hawkins (Judy) witnesses the murder of her boss while she's high above the air doing her singing tightrope-walking act. Without thinking, she tells the Drake gang that she "seen 'em" commit murder, so they chase her out of the circus and into the arms of her special someone, Private J. Wethersby "Pinky" Fothergill (Colonna), who, with Bill's help, cuts Daisy's hair short so she can put on a uniform and hide out in the Army. The police are looking for her, too; they want her to be a material witness against the gang, but Daisy's afraid she won't last long enough to testify. Still, at least Bill's getting an incredible singer for his show, because Daisy's somethin' else! So is the general's daughter, Vicki Marlow (Ann Miller), who can dance like you wouldn't believe.

Daisy manages to keep a low profile for a while, but when she's strong-armed into going with her soldier friends to the only bar in town, the gangsters get wise to this screwy dame after she dances up a storm. When Drake's lowlifes start to take her out by force, her Army buddies fight them off, scaring them away for a bit. But they know she's going to be performing in the big show, and they've got their silencers ready... But Bill has policemen scattered throughout the theater. Even though the bad guys start shooting up the magic act that Pinky and Daisy are attempting to perform, they keep missing their marks. Sharp-shooting Daisy begins returning fire during the finale, and the cops are there to round up the troublemakers and cart them away.

The story was based on the novel *She Loves Me Not* (1933) by Edward Hope, and the play of the same name and year by Howard Lindsay. A 1934 Paramount film, starring Bing Crosby and Miriam Hopkins, had been based on the same sources.

Filmed from December 17, 1941 through January 16, 1942, *Sleepytime Gal* had a serviceable plot, one that was full of intrigue, farce, and music.

Simple Bessie Cobb (Judy) works in the kitchen in a swanky Miami hotel where Chick Patterson (Tom Brown) is in love with Connie Thompson (Mildred Coles). He's got no money but he knows that Bessie can win the talent contest that record company owner Mr. Adams (Thurston Hall) is sponsoring in order to find bandleader Danny Marlowe (Skinnay Ennis) a new vocalist. But Danny's under pressure from the gambler, Honest Joe Kincaid (Harold Huber), that he should choose his "talented" girlfriend, Sugar Gaston (Ruth Terry). When Danny mistakenly thinks Bessie's recording is Sugar's, he sees no problem at all; besides, picking Sugar erases all of Danny's debts to Kincaid. Everything's fine until Sugar's old gangster boyfriend is sprung from jail and wants to plug the girl. The hit men he sends think Bessie is Sugar and they chloroform her mike just as she drowsily croons "Sleepytime Gal" to the radio audience. The bad guys then tote her away and lock her in a deep freeze with "Downbeat" (Jerry Lester), Danny's arranger and the object of Bessie's affections. Sugar herself has been put out of commission by Bessie's three chef friends, but she breaks free of them, running to the hotel where she just might win the contest after all. Chick frees the cold couple in the nick of time, letting Bessie rush in to belt out the winning number. In the end, there are smiles all 'round.

Joan of Ozark (1942) was another of Judy's most entertaining WWII outings, full, as usual, of songs and Nazi thwarting. It was Joe E. Brown's film just as much as Judy's.

Happily singin' and shootin' in the Ozark hills, Judy picks off one quail too many and feels incredibly sheepish when the game warden (Olin Howlin) comes suspicionin' around. Lucky for her, the last bird she shot was a carrier pigeon for an Axis of Evil spy ring. Hailed as a hero in the national press and labeled Public Patriot #1 and "the Hillbilly Mata Hari," Judy knows that she doesn't deserve *any* of the attention for this accident, but wishes like heck she could do *something* significant to help her country. Without knowing it yet again, she has the chance when she's recruited by the angry leader of the foiled spy ring, Phillip Munson (Jerome Cowan), to sing in his New York nightclub (the perfect cover for Nazi evil). That way he can kill her as a warning to all other patriotic Americans. The Third Reich loves the idea, but Munson thinks it's easier and more prudent to use the aggressive talent agent/performer Cliff Little (Joe E. Brown) to secure her employment. But even the pushy Little has a tough time getting her interested in a gig — until he hits on the clever idea of claiming to be with the Department of Justice, and recruits her to be a G-Woman (special agent H2O) to check out a suspected nest of spies at the nightclub. He's heard her sing, so they agree she can go undercover as a singer.

On their way to the club, they accidentally capture their driver, Yamatako (Paul Fung), who had been sent to kill them, thereby adding to Judy's sterling reputation of spy catcher. Instead of closing, Munson decides to use Judy's rep as the perfect cover so they can continue operating. When it's revealed that Cliff's a talent agent, Cliff uses his acting ability to convince Judy that he's really an undercover agent. He disguises himself as a blatantly obvious Nazi spy coming to the club so she can keep an eye on him. The real spies think he's from the Gestapo sent by the Fuhrer himself to check up on their plans. A frightened Cliff plays along, learning more and more about their notion to kill Judy by an explosive champagne bottle that she's using in the morning to christen a new bomber. Too bad that Cliff"s cover is quickly blown by his friend, Eddie McCabe (Eddie Foy, Jr.). Luckily, two FBI agents doubling as Judy's bodyguards, save the agents just in time for Cliff to rush off to save Judy. He needn't hurry — the bomber takes off without Judy being able to hit it. But it's still attached to the plane in a way that will make it impossible for the plane to land without hitting the bottle and blowing everyone up. Cliff and Judy grab an old biplane and somehow manage to get airborne. Judy grabs the bottle and parachutes down, but not before accidentally dropping the bottle — on a Japanese submarine. The commander falls right in her lap. Heroine again!

Ten years later, Eddie visits his friend, surprised to find Cliff (just as much a hick as Judy) and their brood of six youngins...The End.

Highlights of the film include Brown's energetic imitation of Hitler and Judy's singing. Perhaps her best number in the film was "Wabash Blues," giving her that rare opportunity to show off her long, naturally silky hair. *Joan of Ozark* was also notable as Anne Jeffreys' motion picture debut.

Joe E. Brown was supposed to return in *Sleepy Lagoon* (1943), but Dennis Day became Judy's chiropractor-fiancé instead in this Republic political/gambler comedy. The plot involves Judy Joyner (Canova), owner of Sleepy Lagoon's coffee shop, who's been egged on to run for mayor against slimy Cyrus Coates (Will Wright). She wins, but Lancelot Hillie (Day) feels neglected, so she appoints him civilian defense commissioner; hopefully, this will blast him out of their five-year engagement. Her friend Sarah Rogers (Ruth Donnelly) closes all the bars, since the women are certain that such places are the source of Sleepy Lagoon's evil. As a wholesome alternative, they reopen the amusement park. Judy agrees and calls her Uncle Dudley (Ernest Truex) to run the place, him being the head of a large amusement corporation an' all. In truth, he's just a repairman, under the thumb of crooked Joe "Brains" Lucarno (Douglas Fowley) who quickly comes up with the notion of installing gambling tables in the park. The park's a hit! Only two problems: One of Lacarno's henchmen, Lumpy (Joe Sawyer), is making eyes at Judy, and she doesn't seem to mind, much to Lancelot's consternation. Also, Cyrus is still sucking sour grapes, and investigates until he finds something good and dishonest. Brains is arrested but claims that he's been working for Judy all along. Judy knew nothing about it, and Dudley could say so, but Brains is keeping him on ice so that he can't. Judy and Lancelot don disguises, but are still uncovered and chased by the baddies. They manage to find Dudley anyway, but all looks lost when the thugs are about ready to pounce. Enter the hero: Lancelot, and his highly trained female auxiliary militia! The women strike, and clean up the town! Sarah gets Dudley, Lancelot gets his Judy, and the slots get the bird.

Chatterbox (1943) was shot from November 30, 1942 through early January, and was thoroughly Joe E. Brown's picture, though the beautiful Judy had some good song ballads to belt. The showoff "Mad About Him, Sad Without Him, How Can I Be Glad Without Him Blues" by Larry Markes and Dick Charles gave her yodeling a bit of a workout, while "Why Can't I Sing a Love Song?" showed that, in her cute cowgirl outfit, she could be every bit the glamour girl as a Grable or Lamour. This particular Republic Picture also had one of the funniest scripts, from Frank Gill, Jr., including some arresting radio show antics in which Joe and another man have a cowboy fight by smacking themselves in the chests.

Rex Vane (Brown) is the ultimately western hero — on radio. Personal appearances are another matter, as he demonstrates on the eve of becoming a movie star for the first time. Unfortunately for him it's his first time on a horse, and there's a reporter there to capture the frantic antics of Rex letting his spooked horse get away from him. It's Judy Boggs (Canova) what spooked it with her high-pitched singing. But she evens the score

Joe E. Brown and Judy.

by rescuing him, captured by newspaper columnist Carol Forrest (Rosemary Lane) on the front page of all the papers. He's fired from radio, but the head of Mammoth Pictures wants Judy and Rex as a double act in his first picture. Judy wants no part of being a movie star, so Rex gives her a sob story (straight out of one of his radio scripts) about his mother being in the poor house, so what else can she do?

Rex is dumb enough to want to do his own stunts, but is smart enough to know that he can turn his career around if he can figure out a way to rescue *Judy* this time. Since they are dynamiting nearby for the new road, Rex figures that if he invites Judy up to one of the deserted cabins — on a mountain they are *not* blowing up — he can toss a few dyno-caps out the window and save the terrified damsel. Trouble is, Carol switches signs, sending both idiots to the danger zone, and only by the luck of Rex's trusty rope does the couple escape certain death.

CHAPTER SIX

Chet
Returns

Although her film career was going strong, there was still something missing in Judy's life. Then, just like before, the serendipity dripped right in, in the form of Chester B. England.

"Chet returned to Philadelphia, where he was then living," Judy told the press, "and I had almost forgotten about the attractive American who had cheered me that blue evening in London. *Almost* forgotten — but not quite. Not by a big 'quite.' Then I played in Philadelphia, and there he was again, visiting me backstage. He said he had hesitated a long time before coming to see me, because he did not want to presume on such a brief acquaintance. One glance at him was enough to make me want to say that his doubts were completely unjustified. I realized that it had not been mere loneliness that had made him look so good to me in London. I began to be sure it was love at first sight."

By the time her Philadelphia act was over, they had become good friends, finding much in common, laughing at the same things as well. Soon, during a weekend get-together with his family and Anne Canova, Chet popped the question. Judy answered yes, and quickly.

But their engagement was filled with separation, with Judy splitting her time between New York performances and a California film career, and Chet in the army. The first chance they had to see each other during that first long year of engagement was when she was in New York and he was temporarily stationed in Mitchell Field. With a wedding gift of a five-day furlough, the frustrated couple decided to tie the knot and drove up to a little town to marry. They spent their honeymoon in a "swanky New York hotel," Judy said. "Those five days are among the most beautiful souvenirs of our lives."

There was no long honeymoon, but it was apparently long enough. A baby was soon on the way.

Up until her seventh month of pregnancy, Judy was working on her radio show. "I went to a Beverly Hills designer and had him make me a dress with great big shoulder pads and ruffles and stuff. People saw me at the broadcast and on the street and said, 'It's a publicity stunt. She's not going to have a baby.' But honest, I was as big as a truck. I weighed 185 pounds."

War husband Chet had to rush back to his post in U.S. Military Intelligence in Germany. Overseas, he made the papers in 1945, via Judy's publicity machine, by uncovering "the hottest photo record of Nazi secret service agents yet brought to light." Identifying pictures, shot on 16mm film, showed full-face and profile pictures of men and women agents who may have been operating "completely unsuspected" in other countries. His superiors commended him for this work, and he was soon awarded the Bronze Star.*

Chet managed to be there for Tweeny's birth, approximately ten months after receiving the Bronze Star, but he had to leave for overseas just a few days later. "I was born on August 24 in Burbank, CA, at St. Joseph's Hospital," says Julieta, "right across the street from Disney Studios. Don't remember anything about it, but it was 1944; Paris had just been liberated, and I guess there was too much going on to pay attention to another baby wrapped in newspaper."

Judy spent her time doing work for the war effort, and planning for the baby. "It wasn't always easy, but it was better than chewing my fingernails off to the elbow," she said. "Chet and I have only been together about two months since our marriage. He's only seen our daughter for about two days, and that was right after she was born. His letters to me are practically form questionnaires on the progress of the baby. And right now my biggest joy in life is answering these details." Her daily letters back to him "were mostly Julieta stuff." It seems she still had time to write poetry and songs, cook, read, and take the baby to the movies.

The end-of-the-war years were a lonely time for Judy at home, and she made no secret of it, commiserating with all the other war brides. On radio's *Erskine Johnson in Hollywood* (November 29, 1946), she stated, "It was pretty awful. I remember one Thanksgiving I hadn't heard from him for two or three weeks and wondered whether I had anything to be thankful about. Mother, Tweeny's nurse and I had a small turkey but I didn't have much appetite. We took the baby for a ride after dinner and when I got home — there was a telegram from Chet sending me love for Thanksgiving Day. It was a swell day after all. Later he wrote me he had liberated a chicken for the holiday."

Judy's most public (and funniest) revelation about her marriage came when she penned the following article which appeared in February 1946's edition of *Radio Mirror*.

Now that the war is over I'm thinking of writing to President Truman to ask him to declare a National Honeymoon Week.

---

*In 1945, Judy received a citation from the Treasury Department for her work in the most successful bond-selling tour in the East. In fact, sometime during World War II, Judy had been given a tour of the White House by President Franklin D. Roosevelt himself, and she took one of his cigars as a memento. Not quite the Bronze Star, but...

My Chet and I have been married almost three years — of which time the Army has generously allowed us to spend maybe five weeks together. Now that he is coming home to stay I'd like to stop thinking about radio and movies and personal appearances, at least for a while, and concentrate on getting acquainted with my husband.

I'll bet there are thousands of other young Army wives who would get behind such a project — and really make things hot for the government if our legislators turned a deaf ear to romance.

But seriously: the prospect of reunion with my husband is for me, as it must be for so many other wartime brides, a prospect both thrilling and terrifying. Will he have changed?

Or will I? Will I be, in fact, the girl he has been remembering, and writing to, and dreaming of coming home to? What will Chet feel if our fifteen-month-old Tweeny insists that he is not da-da at all; that da-da is that man in the picture frame?

I know there will be adjustments to make, for all three of us — but I'm not afraid. Not really. Our lives together started off too beautifully to be vulnerable now. We will begin by remembering the day on the bridge — then everything will be easy.

The day on the bridge was the day Chet proposed. It was in June of 1942. We had not known one another very long — really *known* one another.

I had met Chet England in London in 1938. I was starring in a show at Café de Paree and was simply miserable with homesickness. When Chet, a boy from back home, came to my dressing room with a mutual friend to meet me, I could have rushed right into his arms. I didn't. I didn't know him and I had to pretend to be a lady, but after he had gone, I found myself wondering whether it was the young man's six-foot-three of beautiful physique, and his blond hair and blue eyes which had bowled me over, or simply the fact that he was a nice young man from Baltimore, Maryland, U.S.A.

We didn't meet again for four years — just a few weeks before the day on the bridge. At that time I was in Philadelphia for a personal appearance, and Chet saw a notice in the papers and came to see me again.

He still looked mighty good to me, so I decided it *had* been the blond hair and blue eyes and the build all the time. Not the homesickness.

Happily, my run at the Earle Theater in Philadelphia was extended, and Chet set to courting me. (Or was it the other way 'round?) When the time came for me to go back to New York, we were warm friends. I hated to go. I had never had so much fun with anybody in two short weeks. Chet's sense of humor, it seemed to me, was something altogether rare and priceless — what would I do if this had all been just an amusing interlude, a few dates because I had been handy, and sort of fun to have around, but nothing to be considered permanent?

This gave me something to worry about for a few days until Chet showed up in New York. He bobbed up regularly for a few weeks. Then he invited my sister and me to spend a weekend with him and his family at their country house outside Philadelphia. A real country weekend was what he promised. If he had any secret notions about letting his parents get a look at the crazy girl he was running around with, he didn't mention them.

We flew down, I with a few secret notions of my own, and some misgivings. (What if they didn't like me?)

I forgot them when I spied Chet waiting at the airport with a station wagon, and as we drove through unbelievably beautiful country toward his home, it seemed to me there was nothing to worry about. Nothing at all. The house was a big, informal, lived-in looking house. And Chet's mother and father were friendly, hospitable people who made us feel immediately at home.

"Now will you relax?" Chet said.

How did he know I hadn't been?

That afternoon, Chet and I slipped away from the others for a little walk.

I was wearing my hair in pigtails, slopping along in flat shoes and no stockings, in a little girlish gingham dress.

Chet said I looked sixteen. I certainly didn't feel like a femme fatale whose milieu is the smoking, smelly insides of a nightclub. I didn't know how I felt, except that whoever I was, whatever my destiny, this moment was terribly close to happiness.

I didn't know where we were walking, but Chet seemed to be leading the way. Suddenly we came upon a singing little stream, rushing along between two lanes of old trees. A narrow handrail bridge led across the water to the farther bank. Chet stopped me halfway across the bridge and asked me to marry him.

There was only one answer to a question like that, asked in such a setting. So he slipped his gold signet ring — the family crest worn smooth by many generations of Englands — onto my engagement finger. And we kissed. It was nice. It was wonderful!

As I think of it, the three years he has been in the Army don't seem long at all.

Judy in 1942.

That quiet, blissful weekend was not a harbinger of what was to come. I flew back to New York and then to Hollywood, and we had to continue our courting by long distance.

In October, Chet went into the Army. We wanted to be married, but there seemed to be no time or place where the Army would put him and my sponsors put me simultaneously.

That went on until March — when, at last, I had New York engagements at the same time that Chet was stationed temporarily at Mitchell Field, L.I. On March 14 we piled Chet's father and a few friends into our car and drove out to Newton, New York, and were married, we *thought*, quietly in the Episcopal Church there. The church looked empty. It just seemed to hum a little. We thought the hum came from outside where a throng of townspeople who had got wind of our plans somehow had collected on the sidewalk. It was not until the ceremony was over that we realized that the balcony of the church was packed to overflowing with kids of all ages.

"I see why you dressed up for the occasion," said Chet, who had worn his private's uniform himself.

"Nonsense," I replied, "for my public I wear shootin' irons."

For Chet I had worn Hattie Carnegie's quietest blue suit, with a navy hat with veil of real Chantilly. I still have the spray of white bouvardia I carried in my white prayer book. The bouvardia is yellow now, and the fragrance has vanished. Looking back I wonder — could it really have been so many moons ago?

We had a five-day honeymoon at the Sherry Netherlands, courtesy of the U.S. Army. After that brief interlude we parted again, I to go back to Hollywood, Chet to go to Ohio State University for training — since he spoke four languages — for service with the A.M.G.

We didn't see one another after that for over a year. In June I tried desperately to fly to Ohio to see him, and was put off six straight planes for lack of a priority. There was not enough time for a train trip across country, so we had to wait until November when Chet had a five-day furlough.

Five days more together — then long months apart. The pattern was getting too familiar to be funny. The next time

I saw Chet was when Julieta, our Tweeny, was two days old. Chet came to see us at St. Joseph's Hospital in the San Fernando Valley (which I had picked because I liked the Disney characters on the walls of the nursery!). He had just four days to admire his new daughter, with hair just as yellow and eyes just as blue as his own, before reporting to Camp Ritchie, MD and boarding a transport heading overseas.

"Tell her her daddy is a master sergeant," Chet said wistfully as he said goodbye. He was very proud of his new stripes.

"A master sergeant in *Intelligence*," I amended his rating, trying to let him know I was proud too, but jokingly so I wouldn't cry.

What a world, I was thinking, to rip people apart when they need most to be together. What a heartless, selfish world to deny its young a chance to be young, and in love, in *peace*.

You get emotional when you've just had a baby, a little hysterical if you aren't careful.

But we survived it. Peace has come — long overdue, but here at last. And we're still young and, God and Time willing, still in love.

That's the thing we're surest of, and that's the thing we're going to count on for all we're worth. That — and the fact that, after all, we've got as much to build on as anyone our age.

Maybe there's a chance yet that we can live like — well, like people.

During Christmas of 1945, it was, as usual, difficult being apart. "Chet was in Strasbourg just before Christmas," Judy said, "and I knew he was homesick and longing to see his baby daughter, Julieta, as much as we wanted him at home. The family tried to make dinner a festive affair, but we couldn't help looking at Chet's vacant chair. In the middle of dinner, the bell rang and a messenger boy delivered a large crate. We opened it to find an oil painting of my husband, done by a famous European, a prisoner of war. Without a word I placed the picture on the vacant chair at the table, and all through dinner, he seemed to be right there with us." She bought him a satin-finished antique desk that was more than 200 years old. From that desk she wrote him V-mail letters every other day, averaging eight pages at a time.

According to Julieta England, "I think what brought my mom and dad together was the old 'opposites attract.' My dad was an intellectual, a cynic, had a wicked sense of humor, and [was] not altogether unattractive. He really did look very much like Marlon Brando did in *Sayonara* when he was younger — but had lost a lot of his hair due to sunstroke. While not full of formal education, my mom was bright and funny, and was most likely a flirt. He was a Yankee, educated in the U.S. and Europe; she was from Florida, a voracious reader and probably didn't have more than the equivalent of a G.E.D. He was an only child; she was one of eight. And then there's the chemical attraction [to] a man in uniform. It would embarrass them both [to hear me say this], but I know they were 'hot and heavy' at times, pulling each other into doorways — possibly desecrating a church or storefront with [their] outrageous behavior."

Havin' some fun with Fili.

CHAPTER SEVEN

Radio Queen

Not busy enough with a film or two a year, and a shiny new marriage, Judy Canova finally got her own regular radio series.

On July 6, 1943, *The Judy Canova Show* opened on the air to announcer, Ken Niles, spieling, "For a breath that's sweet…*(SFX: Hungry panting follows)* and a smile that dazzles *(SFX: Wolf whistle)*, it's Colgate tooth powder! *(Music cue: Piano)* And for a riot of fun, it's America's wacky, wistful, wonderful scatterbrain — Judy Canova!" After more piano music and applause, train noises, and the hootin' an' hollarin' of the cast comes Judy's monologue:

Howdy, ev'rybody! Shore was nice of y'all to come down to the train to meet me. And, boy, am I happy to be comin' back to Rancho Canova. But I shore did have a big time out thar in Hollywood. You know Hollywood. Where men are men and all the girls are married to Charlie Chaplin.

I s'pose y'all's wonderin' what I was doin' in Hollywood. Well sir, I was wonderin' myself there for a while, but I really was out there on a bond-selling tour. I got up on a platform with some of them beautiful gals, movie stars, ya know, and we's givin' away kisses with each bond we sold? I wasn't doin' so good. So finally, I got real mad, I looked 'em all right square in the eyes and I says, "Boys, one kiss from me'll put new life in ya!" Then one feller stepped up an' said he'd buy a $500 bond if I'd kiss his tires.

But really, folks, the most fun I did have on the whole trip was comin' back out here on the train. I ain't never seen so many men and women in uniform in all my life. Why, even the conductor had a wound stripe. A civilian tried to get on.

Ya know, I was really pretty popular on the train, too. This soldier sat around admirin' my travelin' outfit. I guess it was the first time he'd ever seed open-toed Army shoes. And that ain't all that made the eyes bug out either. I also guess it was the first time he'd ever seen a travelin' bag, like the one I was carryin'. My folks gave it to me. It was genuine cow hide. I know it's genuine cow hide cuz it's got four handles on it.

My, but that train sure was crowded. Especially in the women's section. I never did get any sleep. All night long it was pitch and toss, pitch and toss. No wonder. I was sleepin' between two Waves.

But the soldier boys was really wonderful to me. They took a vote and un-a-mously selected me as their pin-up

A promo of Judy gettin' all so-fis-to-cated for radio!

girl. I'da been pinned up there yet if the conductor hadn't helped me down.

Between songs and toothpaste hyping, the slight plot of the premiere show involved getting Judy back to the ranch and showing Ken around the ranch. Mel Blanc was on hand to steal the show with a spitting char-

Doin' her bit for the boys.

acter by the name of Sylvester who spoke *exactly* like his cartoon cat counterpart, wet lisp and all. Once Sylvester drives them to the ranch, Ken wants to "freshen up a bit."

> *Ken:* Where's the bath?
> *Sylvester:* The bath?
> *Ken:* Why, certainly. Don't you have a room with a bath?
> *Sylvester:* No, sir. Out here, we just have a room with a path.

The series became something special over time, hosting one of the best supporting casts in radio history. In sleepy little Cactus Junction, kindly Aunt Aggie (Verna Felton; later, Ruth Perrott), lived with Judy at "Rancho Canova," along with Geranium (Ruby Dandridge), the black maid; Pedro

(Mel Blanc), the Mexican gardener-chauffeur; Mr. Hemingway (Hans Conried), the houseguest who complained about everything; visited sometimes by Joe Crunchmiller (Sheldon Leonard), Judy's no-good boyfriend and cab driver; muscle-bound Humphrey Cooper (Gerald Mohr), double-talking Benchley Botsford (Joe Kearns); and, when needed, Gale Gordon, Elvia Allman, George Niese, and Sharon Douglas rounded out the cast.

Hans Conried and Judy.

One reporter's description of the pre-show (just before recording started) proved that laughs began early every night: "The Canova warm-up starts with genial Howard Petrie introducing the cast members one by one. The sound man accompanies these introductions with appropriate effects — as Verna Felton sits down, the orchestra plays a loud *boom!*; as Hans Conried bows, the sound-effects man rips a cloth. Mel Blanc, who plays 'Pedro,' reels off some of his famous impersonations: Jack Benny's Maxwell, 'Bugs Bunny,' a Hammond organ playing 'Beer Barrel Polka.' Judy

Judy and her horse Penny in Cactus Junction.

herself strolls on in the star spot, red bows on her pigtails, Army shoes on her feet — a perfect picture of a comic-strip hillbilly. The comedienne struts up to the mike in a manner that suggests she's really climbing a high hill, stops and gazes at the audience cheerfully. Just this — and nothing more — sends the audience into an unfailing roar. After the laughter dies down, Judy chats with the folks, asks them to be sure to note her shoes, 'G.I. wedgies,' she calls them. And just before the show goes on the air, she shyly raises her skirt and discloses her favorite garment, baggy striped pantaloons!"

The "hook" of the series was simple — which *The New York World-Telegram* described thusly: "Judy, a homespun lass who talks like Bob Burns, is unlovely and unloved. Most of the jokes arise, one way or another, from these last two circumstances. This is altogether in keeping with radio tradition. If a female of the species expects to call herself a comedienne she must join the tradition of gallant, ugly, unclaimed womanhood."

Judy wasn't quite as man-hungry as, say, a Joan Davis, but she was peckish, and dodged homely insults like a field of cannon fire.

Some of the best guy gags of the series:

Aunt Aggie: You mustn't be discouraged. Remember that in this world, there's a girl for every man and a man for every girl. You can't improve on an arrangement like that.
Judy: Shucks, Aunt Aggie, I don't want to improve on it. I just want to get *in* on it.

Benchley: Do you really believe that nice girls shrink from kissing?
Judy: Shucks, no, if that was true, I'd be nothin' but skin and bones.

Judy (trying to win a date with Van Johnson): You know, the only time I ever saw Van Johnson, I felt just like a bottle of soda pop standin' in the hot sun.
Woman: You did?
Judy: Yeah. I gurgled a little, started to fizz, and then blew my top.

Going on one episode to win a date, she cooed, "I shore would like to go on a long cruise with a movie star. Ooo-wee, how I'd like to park in the dark with Clark, or neck on the deck with Peck."

Salesman: Madame, I think you're going to be difficult to fit.
Judy: Why should I be hard to fit? Shucks, I've got a juvenile figure.
Salesman: Yes, I know, but most of it's delinquent!

Judy: Well, when I was 17 a young feller hugged me and tried to kiss me.
Woman: That's very interesting. And what did you do?
Judy: I did what any real lady would do — I fought him off for about 15 or 20 seconds. As I got older I was able to cut the time down.

It seemed like her friend/maid Geranium had much more luck on the dating front than Ms. Canova, even though the ever-laughing girl was fatter than a whale's parents.

Geranium: Why only last night, my boyfriend, Pomeroy, and I were parked on a dead-end street.
Judy: What happened, Geranium?
Geranium: We brought that street back to life!

Geranium: My boyfriend, Pomeroy, calls me his little honey waffle.
Judy: Why does he call you that?
Geranium: The more honey he uses on me, the mushier I get.

Judy: Tell me somethin'; is Pomeroy a wolf, Geranium?
Geranium: Oh, *no*, Ms. Judy! He's a gentleman among gentlemen!
Judy: Gentleman among gentlemen?
Geranium: Yeah, but just don't turn him loose among women.

Geranium: We wuz two-thirds married last summer.
Judy: Two-thirds married?
Geranium: Yes, ma'am, I was there, the preacher was there, but Pomeroy never showed up.

It could've been that weight problem that kept her from getting anywhere with Pomeroy. Judy was always ready to listen to the woman's problems, and tried to help.

Judy: Geranium, you oughta try to reduce.

Geranium: Oh, I am, Miss Judy. I go to a combination beauty parlor and dress maker.

Judy: A combination beauty parlor and dress maker to *reduce?*

Geranium: Yessum. The slogan is, "If we can't take it off, we'll hide it for ya."

Judy: You're always exaggeratin' about yer figure. Shucks, you gotta lotta nice curves.

Geranium: Curves? Honey, most of them are practically u-turns!

"Let me hear y'all!"

Pedro was easily the most popular sidekick, usually stealing whatever scene he crept in on, with what became his highly popular opening line: "Pardon me for talking in your face, señorita." The timid, heavily accented little man was sure one unlucky buck, especially in the art of love.

> *Pedro:* Señorita, I tried to elope with my girl last night.
> *Judy:* You did, Pedro?
> *Pedro:* Si. I put a ladder up to my girl's window, but her father caught me when I was halfway up the ladder.
> *Judy:* Golly, what'd you do?
> *Pedro:* What could I do? I painted the side of the ho-ws. *(Big audience laugh)* Señorita, I like to neck with my girl. She always says her keeses will send me.
> *Judy:* Do they?
> *Pedro:* No, I'm too smart to go. *(Audience loves it)* Well, *hasta mañana*, señorita.
> *Judy:* A tasty banana to you too, Pedro.

It wasn't just his pedestrian pace that kept him as the "slowest Mexican" on radio. This guy was two enchiladas short of a combo.

> *Judy:* Oh, hello, Pedro. Say, you look sleepy today.
> *Pedro:* I am, señorita. I snored so loud last night, I kept waking myself up.
> *Judy:* Well, if you snored so loud, why didn't you do somethin' about it?
> *Pedro:* I deed. I moved to another ro-om.
> *Judy:* Pedro, you got up *awfully* late this morning. Didn't your alarm clock go off?
> *Pedro:* Si, the alarm clock rang, alright, but the trouble was, it went off while I was slee-ping.

Mel Blanc (the voice of Bugs Bunny and all things Warner Bros.) *loved* being on the show with all his voice pals, and wrote in his autobiography that "Judy wasn't any more of a hillbilly than Gracie Allen was a dizzy dame...Judy was actually a fine singer with a great range..."

Since, as ever, the theme of her show was *country*, Mel joined her on another popular segment. She would often tell of the visits with her kinfolks, or about her relations, and the audience ate it up. Mel Blanc made a great "Pa."

Ma: Wake up, Pa. Ya lazy critter.

Pa: (Yawns) Have I been sleeping long, Ma? What time is it?

Ma: July 1936. The 4th of Ju-ly parade is a-goin' by the house, Pa. It's right purdy.

Pa: I shore wish I was facin' the street. *(Big audience laugh)*

Ma: Git up, Pa. Don't you know the early bird catches the worm?

Mel Blanc gets a workout while Judy cracks the whip between rehearsals.

Pa: Gosh, do we need meat that bad? *(Big audience laugh)*
What's fer breakfast, Ma?
Ma: I don't rightly know, Pa.
Pa: Oh. Hash again, huh? *(Big audience laugh)*

Judy popularly proved that humor could be simple as heck. Also, there was often that subtle battle of wits — country girl vs. Hollywood types — that leveled the playing field for everyone.

Opera Director: Where have you been singing lately?
Judy: In the bathtub.
Opera Director: What is your favorite aria?
Judy: The north end of the tub.

Judy: This is my brother Zeke, Mr. Kent. He sort a' looks out for me.
Kent: Oh, your bodyguard, eh?
Judy: Yeah…Zeke knows some durn cute tricks. Why, he kin bust a man's arm just by shakin' hands with him.
Kent: How cunning.
Judy: Yes, sir. Zeke, shake hands with Mr. Kent.

Judy did have a wealth of high-falutin' singing talent to break up the monotony of laughs. An audience favorite was always the impressive yodel work she pitched between lively songs. Still, it was the belly laughs that got her in good with radio audiences.

In 1947, *Variety*'s Jack Hellman wrote a short treatise on the amount of laughter in situation comedy of the day. He measured "studio laugh volume," putting it at between 70 and 80%, the highest registered by Judy's show at 81%. The average laugh lasted 4.1 seconds. The general spread was 3.2 seconds long. In 1946 Judy had received 250,000 fan letters and responded with 150,000 pictures, which cost her a nickel apiece ($7,500).

September 2, 1947's regular *Variety* review was even more complimentary, stating that "it's a joke show most of the way, but unlike most comics, Canova doesn't monopolize the laugh lines. Wide play is given the versatility of Blanc and Kearns, and occasionally Judy is the foil off whom the punch lines carom. There's not a better line reader or straight singer than the back-woodsy cut-up, and she lets the laughs fall where they may. It all makes for a smartly tailored job with little need for alterations."

This was the same year she won the Erskine Johnson (Hollywood columnist and commentator) Achievement Award for her comedy success. He awarded it to her on his radio show on February 1, 1947.

"Funnily" enough, it was also around this time that the Gagmasters Institute of New York City announced the findings of a nationwide poll in which 2500 amateur and professional gag writers named Jack Benny as America's top comedian, and Judy as best comedienne.

Victor Borge, Judy and Benny Goodman during the radio years.

Not *everyone* appreciated the series, as the biased *Daily Worker* in New York wrote that her series was the worst comedy on the air, deriving most of its humor from offensive, outdated stereotypes. "There's Pedro, the Mexican chauffeur, portrayed as lazy, stupid and lascivious (half of the 'laughs' in the show come from the sound of his accent), and Geranium, a foppish old Negro 'mammy' given the worst sort of Uncle Tom lines."

The Canovas guesting with Don Ameche on radio.

In a sense it was true, but it was unfair to say that's where the majority of the laughs came from. Judy's series was no worse or different than what other shows were doing at the time, especially in their portrayals of black and minority servants. Even Mel Blanc found himself defending his Pedro accent when applying it here, and later to his Speedy Gonzalez cartoons.

The following article, originally included in an NBC promotional booklet, provides a colorful, behind-the-scenes look at the popular radio program.

Early Saturday afternoons the stage of NBC's Holly-wood Studio A is brilliantly lighted, but practically empty. Before the big mulberry colored curtain with the sparkling cutout letters announcing "The Judy Canova Show," a few shirt-sleeved musicians idly stand by, chewing on apples or drinking Cokes. Their leader, Charles (Bud) Dant, saunters in and, once on the podium, exhorts the members of the orchestra present, to remember to make the last line of a song either E-flat or B-flat when they run through it again. They all nod solemnly.

Members of the famous Sportsmen Quartet, also shirt clad, pore over a battered copy of a morning newspaper, [as] sound effects technician (Bob Conlan) slowly strolls in. An actual show rehearsal seems quite remote.

Suddenly, a jacket-clad Judy, her hair in a ribbon and a song sheet in her hand, bounces on stage. As though by a signal, the musicians slide into their seats and pick up their horns. More musicians step from behind the back curtains, put out their cigarettes, and take their places behind piano, harp, drums, and bass. The Sportsmen abandon their newspaper and congregate at the mike.

No downbeat is given, not a hand is raised in signal, but somehow the first song of the show is started, with Dant's band right on beat as Judy lustily warbles, "If I Could Be One Hour with You." During the singing, a cast magically materializes on stage.

Watching Judy Canova clown through an ad-libbing of the lines in the script's situation comedy is sheer entertainment, but add Hans "Hemmingway" Conried, Mel "Pedro" Blanc, Gale "Dodge" Gordon, happy, big Ruby "Geranium" Dandridge, and you have a full recipe for riotous goings-on.

An on-looker's attention must eventually wander to the musicians. More than once during the hour Judy and her complement of comedians run through the roles of the socially aspiring "unacceptable" and her snooty neighbors, "the Dodges." The music-makers, who've played on countless comedy shows and have watched many a comic rise and fall, pay Judy and her cast the greatest compliment possible just by their lack of raucous laughter. They sit quietly cradling their instruments in their arms, goggling at the antics of the show's participants. Their inward mirth is revealed only by the amused expressions on their faces.

The comedy routines outlined in the script are given that inimitable, personal touch when Judy and her co-workers add a few priceless ad-libs. All in all, rehearsal is an enter-taining hour of fun. One wonders how all this hilarity can be telescoped into the allotted twenty-nine minutes and thirty seconds of air time.

Able, balding Joe Rines, the producer of the NBC show, explains it this way, "Y'see, these old troupers have clocks inside their heads. They can boil the show down to a half hour without so much as a sidewise glance at the studio clock.

"But you would be surprised how few changes, outside of their clothes, are made between rehearsal and the actual audi-ence performance. Many of the humorous asides and gags that Judy and the cast make during rehearsal are incorpo-rated into the airshow. No one who hears 'The Judy Canova Show' misses anything that goes on in rehearsal, really. They just miss the fun of seeing it."

At some point in the 1940s Judy toured with *The Judy Canova Show*. This allowed audiences all over the country a chance to see a different kind of radio presentation, one heavy on the visuals. The show was pro-duced and directed by William H. King, with musical direction by Frank Konyi. The format of this special program ran as follows:

Overture

Canova Capers, featuring the Ann Garri Dancers and The Five Taylors

Bert Henderson, "The Man Who Proves People Are Funny"

Fid Gordon & Co.

JUDY CANOVA

The Canova Guest Ranch, featuring Pansy the Horse, Robert and Renee, and the Ann Garri Dancers

JUDY CANOVA

Gayety on Wheels, featuring Joe Mole

THE CANOVAS — JUDY, ANNE and ZEKE
GRAND FINALE

A description in the tour book states, "The ludicrous antics of Pansy the Horse furnish one of the highlights of the touring Judy Canova Show. With clever and attractive Marie Mayo playing the part of the trainer, this lively two-manpower creation proves that even a factory-bred horse can be successful as an outstanding comedian if it has the right kind of stuff inside it. The Pansy the Horse act has been in the possession of the Mayo family for more than 65 years, and is world famous in entertainment circles. It was first brought over to this country from Germany many years ago by Marie Mayo's father, who had cavorted with the whimsical Pansy through all the leading variety halls of Europe."

The Ann Garri Dancers had appeared in films such as *Blue Skies, Emperor's Waltz, Viennese Moon*, while Joe Mole was reportedly the "greatest bicyclist in the world," still riding his tricycle at age 67. The trampoline act Robert and Renee had toured with Spike Jones and were also part of Olsen & Johnson's *Hellzapoppin'* show.

According to information at the time, Anne supervised all musical arrangements and Judy's "special material" on the tour.

CHAPTER EIGHT

Family and Film

A hit radio series made Judy just that much more in demand for films. And 1944's *Louisiana Hayride* was one of her best offerings during the war years — another bright, fast, behind-the-Hollywood-scenes vehicle that ran 67 minutes, with nary a pause in the jokes.

It begins with Judy Crocker (guess who?) buying her aunt and uncle an auto camp/rooming house in Cedarview, before boarding the train back to her home in Glen Falls. On the journey, she meets a couple of slick characters, J. Huntington McMasters (Richard Lane) and Canada Brown (George McKay), looking for someone to bilk. They don't pay attention to her, even though she's wallowing in cash due to an oil company taking a generous option on her farm land. Because she's got so *much* money, she's calling the stash of cash with her "chicken feed." Once they figure out her slang, they dart quickly for her place, posing as salesmen for a plastic shoe stock. Judy and all her bumpkin friends hate wearing shoes, so the ever-resourceful McMasters (after hearing Judy sing), switches cons to announce that he and his partner are really motion picture producers. McMasters goes on to wow the female bumpkin with a pitch for a new picture; its title, "Louisiana Hayride." Convinced by this potential blockbuster idea, Judy and her family decide to make an investment. The bogus producers gladly take her dough and live the high life in Hollywood — until Judy shows up, determined to force the crooks to take more of her money as a further investment. In order to string this golden goose along, the duo enlists the help of an intelligent bellboy, Gordon Pearson (Ross Hunter), who wants to be a movie director, to pose as *Judy's* director. The tables are turned when Gordon uses Judy's money to actually *produce* a film. Renting a studio and camera, the conmen are forced to go along with the plan, or Gordon will tell their pigeon the truth.

"Fifteen hundred dollars for a night watchman?" McMasters complains to the studio owner. "We'll probably be here ourselves every night."

"*That's* why we need a night watchman," the owner admits.

Pearson also hires Montague Price (Lloyd Bridges) to rewrite the script, but during filming Price realizes that the entire plot is identical to a current Broadway play, and that stops the film production cold. Luckily, Judy's Maw Crocker (Minerva Urecal) has been right friendly with a nervous little man by the name of Malcolm Cartwright (Hobart Cavanaugh) since they've been in Hollywood. Malcolm likes what they've shot so far, and reveals himself to be the producer of that pesky Broadway play. He offers Judy and family free motion picture rights as a present. The conmen are hauled away by the police, and Judy finds herself without any oil on her land, but on the verge of stardom. And that's where the picture ends.

Nineteen-forty-four was also the year that Judy landed a song in *some-one else's* soundtrack. She, Harry Tobias, Zeke Canova and Eddie Dean had all collaborated on "Don't Turn Me Down, Little Darlin'" which ended up in PRC Pictures' *I'm from Arkansas*, starring Slim Summerville and El Brendel.

Also around this time Judy collected up a mess of honorary titles: she was made a colonel in Kentucky, a sheriff in Texas and a fire-chief in Boston.

It wasn't all good news, however. On August 15, 1944, "Juliette" signed a contract to sever Harry Canova as her manager, stating the following formal reasons:

Undue influence exerted by you, including undue influence exerted by you as a result of the confidential relationship existing between us.

Failure of consideration; and lack of consideration.

Breach by you of your obligations to me by virtue of the fiduciary relationship between us.

Violation by you of your fiduciary obligation to me.

The invalidity and illegality of said managerial agreement.

Plus a slew of "failure to comply's" with various California laws and regulations put forth by the Screen Actors Guild and the American Federation of Radio Artists. Monies paid were also demanded back.

With all that money coming in, she had to look out for herself. She liked spending it, too. One of her hobbies was collecting rare and beautiful 18th century fans, many of which were bejeweled. Some were valuable museum pieces, some were framed in her home; one of them had been the property of a Chinese princess, and another had belonged to Dolly Madison.

The letterhead off Judy's own stationery.

Family life with Judy, Fili, and Tweeny.

Tweeny and Judy.

She also loved to cook, and had an impressive collection of cookbooks. She was almost famous for it, leading to many fans sending her additions to her collection which she kept in a huge panel of bookshelves in her sitting room den. Diana says, "I spent the morning down in my basement looking for what I realized doesn't exist. I called my sister who packed it all up (22 years ago) and got the answer I figured I would get. Mom for years always talked about 'when she wrote her book...' Trouble is, she never started it. No diaries. No letters. She wrote down RECIPES! She loved food, had a million cookbooks, and tirelessly wrote down recipes from places and people she loved. But as far as writing down anything about her life? *Nothing.* We have a million pictures. I have a huge plastic container of her scrapbooks from vaudeville that weren't damaged by a flood in her living room.

"I had found an old book with all this writing in it and thought I had struck pay dirt, only to find a friend of hers had written poetry in it page after page, and then Mom took over and wrote, guess what? MORE RECIPES! I have all of her scripts from her radio show, but no notes of hers. She never wrote a lengthy letter to either one of us."

In 1947 the press announced that Judy was to compile a "Canova Cookbook" from the 30,000 recipes she had collected. It would only be the ones she had personally tested, and have an index system that "really takes the headache out of trying to find the recipe you want."

She also liked taking 16mm home movies, and spent a good deal of time filming Tweeny's month-by-month growth.

Meanwhile, back at Columbia Pictures...

Hit the Hay (1945)'s working title of *Hayfoot, Strawfoot* doesn't seem to fit the 62-minute opera spoof either, considering the farcical plot. Judy Stevens (Canova), daughter of famed and departed opera diva Madge Stevens, has a beautiful voice and is wasting it churning out arias whilst milking cows in the local farmers' market where she works. The local opera company is in trouble because their usual tycoon, J. Bellingham Parks (Paul Stanton), refuses to give any more money to such a profitless business. The only way managing director Roger Barton (Francis Pierlot) and his son Ted (Ross Hunter) are going to prime the pump again is by finding another Madge Stevens. Ted gets lucky when he hears Judy sing, but in trying to save his star worker from leaving, the market owner, Mr. Frisby (Louis Mason) offers Judy no raise — just a pound of butter a week; plus two pounds of bacon.

"But with your name in lights, you'll make thousands of friends," Ted claims.

"But with two pounds of bacon, I'll make *millions* of friends," Judy checkmates.

Oddly, when auditioning for all the opera bigwigs, she's given a pop ballad to croon, devoid of operatic acrobatics. Still, she wows them just the same. Parks agrees to put money back into the company, but he's upset when he discovers how she was discovered. So she's unveiled to the press as a simple farm girl, daughter of Madge Stevens. That doesn't improve her social graces. When one reporter asks if her favorite composer is Mozart, she replies, "Oh not really; he used to be, but not no more. What's he written lately?"

The trouble is, Mimi Valdez (Gloria Holden), former diva of the company, has it in for poor Judy, wangling Judy's true origin out of Parks' secretary, the timid Wilbur Whittlesey (Grady Sutton), and blackmails Ted to giving her the lead role. Locking Mimi in the closet does the trick temporarily, but it doesn't solve the fact that Judy just can't act. So they've rigged it so that Judy sings behind the scenes while a true lookalike struts the stage. All goes well, but Judy hates the deception. Luckily Ted's girlfriend and reporter, Sally Mansfield (Doris Merrick), gets the idea to praise Judy's comedic ability, giving her an idea of what to do for the next opera.

Enter "Tillie Tell" based on Rossini's *William Tell*, taking place during the 1825 "Annual Apple Shoot" in which Judy demonstrates her true calling — bein' a hoot an' a hollar, complete with an updated '40s score (of course with tunes from the overture) for the whole opera company. Lots of high singin' for Tillie, which at first the bluebloods don't dig, but soon everyone's hep! During the second act with "the Lone Ranger theme" set to a swingin' beat, Tillie keeps shooting at Mario Alvini (Fortunio Bonanova). The drummer keeps shaking his head to indicate that she's missed, and Fortunio keeps putting bigger apples on his head until she makes it. The show's a bona fide hit, and even Mario agrees to marry her.

Variety's review of *Hit the Hay* stated that Judy Canova fans would find it "adequate film fare due to her standard antics and hillbilly corn. Direction isn't so hot but swing-the-classics plot manages chuckles along the way." *The Hollywood Reporter* was a little less enamored, admitting that "it's all in good, clean fun, of course, and the reason *Hit the Hay* won't hit any but the lesser spots is that old plaint — the thin is spread too thick and the few worthwhile ideas stretched to the bustin' point... the plot is strictly from corn, aged but not blended. Yet, as for Judy, shucks, she's still our favorite ear-ritant."

To mark the conclusion of *Hit the Hay's* finish, a gala party was given by Ross Hunter in Sam Steiffel's opulent home, which was decorated to resemble a barn. As celebrities Frank Sinatra, Joan Davis, Rudy Vallee,

Bonita Graville, Janet Blair, and many others entered in western attire via a hay wagon, there were pigs to the right of them, chickens to the left, and donuts dangling from the ceiling.

At this time she was in Hooper's top 15 rating for her Saturday night radio series. "There are 22 in the band and 45 people to run," Judy said of her hectic career, "as the show belongs to me. That's a lot to keep me busy."

In 1945 one of the most rampant (and untrue) news stories had Judy inheriting a 40-room villa and a 500-acre farm in Possagno, Italy, from her artistic ancestor, Antonio Canova. "But I'd never heard of him," Judy admitted at the time. "So I went to the public library and looked him up. And sure enough, there was a lot of stuff about him. He was quite a guy. He's the man who sculpted 'The Three Graces.' Unfortunately it's well-known mostly because the name is so handy to tack on trios of bathing beauties who are anything but!" The letter telling her of the inheritance was first sent to her aunt, Angela Canova, in Jacksonville, Florida. It was signed by Carmine Bitettie and said her uncle, Enrico Canova, had died in Italy during the war and left her his estate on 500 pristine acres.

"I'd love to sing 'Romeo and Juliet' from one of those balconies," Judy said, "but I wouldn't give up my American citizenship if they'd promise me the whole Italian boot. And that's probably what I'd get, too, once they heard me yodel." The reported catch was that she would have to live on the estate. Rather than move out of Hollywood, she signed the entire property over to the Italian government to use as a hospital or school.

At least, that was the *studio press release* version. In reality, there was no Italian villa on Judy's horizon. What prompted the story, and its purpose, remains a mystery.

Soon after, Judy was tempted to start a yacht club on her considerable beach property in the Jacksonville area. At the same time, she made the papers again with her desire to restage Gershwin's *Girl Crazy*, "tailored to her needs" by radio writer Opie Cates, and with Dale Evans lured away from Republic for at least a season. This idea remained exactly that — an idea.

After *Hit the Hay*, Judy also intimated that her next picture would be a horror-western with Peter Lorre and Boris Karloff playing ghost town spooks. "But it's only at the discussion stage," she told reporters. "I'm afraid to even talk about it for fear it won't be filmed. But it's a wonderful idea."

It was, and it wasn't.

She needed some time off. A vacation to Mexico City, then an air tour of South America sounded good. "I have a commitment to make a picture for Columbia," she said, possibly referring to the Karloff project, "and I am trying to have it arranged so I won't be working in July

and August when I'm on my air tour. That would give me two months
to make the tour. It's something I've looked forward to for a long time.
The last picture I made for Columbia was *Hit the Hay*, and most of that
was during July and August, so I ended up the year with exactly ten
days off. I had to use that for a bond tour to New York. It wasn't much
of a vacation."

Still, she signed on — as did Jack Haley, Dale Evans and others — for
a giant benefit show to raise funds for a monument to be erected for the
28 entertainers who were killed while on USO tours in the battle theaters of the world.

She was also "running" for honorary mayor of Studio City in May of
1946, against actress Bonita Granville and announcers Ken Niles and Bill
Goodwin. As she wrote in *Hollywood Nite Life* on April 19, 1946:

> Well folks, as you probably know, I'm running for honor-
> ary mayor of Studio City. Yes sir, I'm throwing my hat into
> the political ring and it's a lovely John Frederics model with
> a pickle in the middle and mustard on top.
>
> I'm going to put my shoes on and run on a solid American
> platform made of slightly used lumber recently rejected by
> the FHA. My ticket is non-partisan and entitles voters to a
> free, round-trip hitch-hike to Azusa and all points west.
>
> If elected, I can safely say without fear of contradiction
> that I will not view with alarm, nor point at with undue
> pride anything from the rockbound coasts of the Los Ange-
> les River to the sunny slopes of Sunnyslope Avenue.
>
> When I take office, I will immediately ask for four curbs
> on Ventura Boulevard instead of two, so there will be more
> room to park.
>
> Indeed, I promise to hold the line on price control, ter-
> mite control and remote control. In fact, I expect to be left
> holding the line.
>
> If any critter wants to start blowing the lid off ceilings, he
> can sure enough start in his own home.
>
> I will ask for a five-day week, with good time and a half
> for overtime.
>
> My agricultural program is strictly corn and more corn.
> All valley farmers will be Gentlemen Farmers, in fact, even
> their scarecrows must change to evening clothes at dusk.
>
> We will install a brand new jailhouse that will be the most
> exclusive in the country. Before being booked, a criminal will

have to take three screen tests before we hang his picture in the Rogue's Gallery.

Little business men must also be aided, but I frankly don't know how to keep the wrestlers from ending up on the flat of their backs.

So remember, every vote you cast for Judy Canova means four votes for Judy Canova, 'cause my Uncle Wardheeler was a taxidermist and he taught me how to stuff a ballot-box.

Singin' in the Corn (1946) was one of Judy's funniest films of the decade, thanks to sidekick Allen Jenkins and a few comic numbers. Filmed for Columbia Pictures under the working title of "Ghost Town," the plot involves Judy McCoy (Canova), carnival soothsayer, inheriting a fortune and the musty old town of McCoy's Gulch from her grandfather. But before she can lay her hands on the money, she has to give the Gulch back to the Native Americans from whom he originally stole it — and within 24 hours, no less. If she fails in her assignment, Honest John Richards (Alan Bridge), Grandpa McCoy's former business partner, gets his grubby hands on it. Richards and his no-good boys have the Indians convinced that the town is haunted, but she and her carnival partner, Glen Cummings (Jenkins), finally succeed in shaking a confession out of the bad guys by threatening to drown them. The Indians take the property, and Judy's in the money.

Judy had four songs in this one: "Pepita Chiquita," "An Old Love Is a True Love," and "I'm a Gal of Property" by Allan Roberts and Doris Fisher, and "Ma, He's Making Eyes at Me" by Sidney Claire and Con Conrad.

She was set to have a part in Tom Breneman's first film, *Breakfast in Hollywood* (1946), interviewing and showcasing many acts, like a brilliant one from Spike Jones. But it wasn't to be. And worse news was to follow.

Pete Canova — close friend, manager, brother — died in June of 1947. According to Julieta, "I was about three when Pete passed away. We never did get the true story of why he wasn't in the [musical] group. Pete and his wife, Florence ('Fauncie'), had an adopted daughter, Floretta — a combination of Florence and Henrietta (Pete and Judy's mother) — and after Pete died, Florence remarried and her new husband adopted Floretta."

Judy was given the title of Honorary Postmaster when she became Queen of the National Association of Postmasters' 1947 convention in Los Angeles. For entertainment, she was joined by the Hoosier Hotshots, The Texas Rangers, Ken Curtis, and Carolina Cotton. Fifteen hundred postmasters, plus two special Union Pacific trains loaded with 1,000 delegates, attended the five-day meeting. She was joined by her sister Anne and brother Zeke, reviving their old act.

Later that year she also offered a voice scholarship to some young gifted performer at the Santa Barbara Music Academy, headed by the renowned Lawrence Tibbett.

Pete Canova.

Judy Canova filled in a *lot* of her off-time with a variety of causes. She was named "March of Dimes Girl of 1948" for her active charity work. She said at the time, "Although the official [fund] drive is over, we mustn't forget the fight against infantile paralysis the rest of the year. The disease doesn't take a nine- or ten-month layoff, so neither should we." It was reported that she was going to make a series of shorts for March of Dimes,

Gettin' ready!

too. She appeared on various radio shows as a guest star between January 14th and 31st to continue the MOD campaign, and also "floated" in a few MOD parades. More than 1,500 transcription discs of her special 1949 show were circulated to stations (240 cities) throughout the country. Governor Thomas J. Mabry of New Mexico declared January 30th as "Judy

Canova March of Dimes Day" in Albuquerque. Annie and Zeke were also there to round out the trio; more than 1500 people were turned away from the sold-out proceedings in the Laloma Auditorium that Saturday night.

When fans sent in their dimes for a signed photo of Judy, she would turn the money over to the National Foundation for Infantile Paralysis. In 1949 the children's ward in the new hospital planned for the atomic

Playing for charity.

project in Pasco, Washington, was to be named after Judy in appreciation of her singing at the foundation's first benefit performance.

In 1948 alone, she could be found yodeling for the boys at the Sawtelle Veterans' hospital, performing with the Future Farmers of America in Kansas City (and in Chicago) for two thousand 4-H youngsters, and handing out lollipops to kids in New York City's Bellevue hospital. She received a pig from the Future Farmers of America to thank her for appearing at two of their conventions. The pig escaped from its crate and two writers had to chase it for a mile into Beverly Hills, where it was finally caught feasting on Mary Pickford's expensive garbage.

In private life, Judy was the opposite of her characteristic rube-like behavior and dress, opting for the latest dresses and glamorous hairstyles of the day. "When I'm in costume I feel like I'm 10 years old," she told the *L.A. News* in 1948. "Which is five years younger than I really am." But left to herself, she would often be seen privately in more comfortable clothes — for studio rehearsals, a grey wool jumper with a Roman striped casual blouse with convertible V-neck collar, long full sleeves and deep cuffs, with slacks, shorts, or tailored suits.

In December of 1948 she returned home to find a divorce being sought by Chet; along with that bombshell was his claim for community property. *The Los Angeles Herald* wrote, "Many friends felt that Judy Canova and Chet England would call off their rift at Christmas. It wasn't to be, but they did spend the day together with their youngster. Judy is off to the South any minute to attend the inauguration of Governor-Elect Fuller Warren of Florida."

Judy finally divorced England because, as one report states, "his constant sarcasm made her too nervous to work" and he frequently sulked and stayed away from home. Another source stated that the conflict of their careers caused the breakup, and that Chester soon moved out of their North Hollywood home. Judy hoped their differences would be settled, and that he would move back in.

Julieta England recalls, "My mom and dad were divorced when I was very young, so what I remember of him was that I only saw him on weekends as I grew up. My first real memory of him was him standing in our kitchen talking to our maid/mammy, Alma. I clearly remember sitting in a chair and then taking his hand and walking out to his car.

"Then, when my mom married my stepfather, and my dad moved to New

York from California, I saw him only during the summers. We'd write, and when his work moved him back to California, I'd see him more often. He was brilliant, in the foods industry, and fluent in several languages. He and I became much closer as I got older, and [by the time] he passed away [in 1980], we had been best friends for a number of years. He remarried and he and his wife adopted two girls. I was never close with either of them, and I always felt that my stepmother resented the fact that my dad made a place in his life for me.

"Since my parents divorced when I was so young, I never saw any arguments, never heard a bad word about my mom from him. She, on the other hand, was not shy about being critical about everything he said and did when he and I spent time

Above: Christmas with the Canovas.
Below: At the beach!

together. I remember the first Christmas at our house in Beverly Hills — the preceding summer in Florida my mother and stepfather had met a man from Montana. Turns out he owned Christmas-tree farms, and would cut and drive them down to Southern California by the truckload. He promised them a tree for the new house, and it turned out to be almost 20 feet tall. The ceiling in the living room was only 18 feet, so the bottom had to be cut down. Naturally, a tree that tall was also *very* wide. It held a very prominent place at the end of our living room. When my Dad walked in to pick me up for a Christmas visit, he looked at it and said, 'What's Radio City doing for a tree this year?' My stepdad laughed; my mother got irritated."

An early shot of the trio on radio.

CHAPTER NINE

Records
and Such

In 1949 Judy Canova was voted "Queen of the Air." It was reported that in 1948 she was getting $11,000 a week for her fall show, which would drop down to $8,000 in 1949. She was feeling the effects of the March of Dimes tour, too. Her Hooper rating shot up 2.7 points to 15 and her Nielsen rating went from 4 to 13, a marker of 5.6 above her previous popularity. Functioning as executive producer of the show, she had

Signin' for the fans.

to pay her writers (Fred Fox, Henry Hoople, and Artie Phillips), directors, musicians, actors, and others out of that $11k. She also employed a practice not common in radio — after the Saturday broadcast, the entire cast staged a preview of next week's show. "This gives us a week to get rid of the rough spots," she explained.

Yet even with all that money rolling in, she didn't lose site of the people. She kept performing as much as possible, even at county fairs. She was the feature attraction at the 30th annual Mississippi Valley Fair in August of 1949. It was the sort of show for which she was famous — plenty of comedy and music — with tickets just a buck for adults and 50 cents for kids (the same admission prices as her radio performances).

She was playing a lot of fairs at the edge of 1950, and even entertained the notion of going back on the Broadway stage for producer Paul Feigay. He envisioned the possibility of the star stepping away from her hillbilly persona: "Such a change of pace — and she could handle it easily — would give much more scope to her career." The show was to be *Nightingale Nell*, based on the "Swedish Nightingale," Jenny Lind.

When asked if she'd like to do a straight role for a change, she answered, "I don't think I'm the type. People like me in the type of roles I've been doing and I think they'd be shocked if I did something else. But, you know,

there's always a third act in life. Anything can happen."

Almost to prove the point, she turned to recording.

On December 13, 1948 her single "Go to Sleepy, Little Baby" from Mercury Records hit the shelves. The following month the National Babysitters Club of Chicago chose it as their 1949 theme song. During the course of just one year it was translated into four languages.

Two years earlier she had a modest hit with "Apple on a Stick"/"My Fickle Eye" which one review reported as being "blessed with clever lyrics, catchy tunes and danceable rhythms." For the A-side, she did the second chorus in a high Baby Snooks voice, which threw the band and spoiled one take when they had to stop to laugh.

Of course a hit single has to lead to a full album, hence *The Judy Canova Souvenir Album* was born and released by Decca in January 1949, which included, "You Don't Have to Say You're Sorry," "I Was Wrong," "Goodnight, Soldier," and "You Sang My Love Song to Somebody Else." These were popular ballads that Judy sang at Army hospitals during the war. *Billboard* wrote that "Canova fans will go for this set, but to others its hybrid nature will be disappointing. Gal sings with fine hill-country flavor, but her backing is slick, big-city stuff that doesn't blend. Her affect-ingly simple sincerity is meant for the sob set, but the jazzy working, with trumpets, saxes, etc. actually seems to make fun of her efforts. The cover photo is a highly glamorized job that further attempts to separate the gal from her character."

Now that early television was cutting into radio's power, it's possible that Judy was looking around for new ways of keeping busy. She talked with anyone who had a credible idea. British producer Jack Hylton wanted her in the summer of 1949 as the lead for his new musical show, *Hillbilly in London*, written by Jarvis Davis and Philip Swallow, which he hoped to do as a motion picture. She was also planning to tour in a revival of *Come Out of the Kitchen*, a play that Ruth Chatterton once made a hit. Judy wanted to try it out in smaller areas before touring the East and South with it.

To battle TV in the meantime, she came up with the novel approach of getting some attention back to the airwaves. She wanted to create an Academy of Radio Arts and Sciences, patterned after the Motion Picture Academy, an organization that would hand out "Mikes" instead of "Oscars." When plans were drawn up, she invited radio industry management and unions to have a peek. "This is no time for radio to sit back and take things for granted," she said in 1949, "not with television making the strides that it is. Radio should take stock of itself, work for improvement and give the public the best." She was soon joined by Jimmy Durante, with "Schnozzola" specifically requesting that script writers get more due.

It was, of course, a losing battle, with not much fight.

Other news of the year: on March 10, 1949, Judy was ninth in the top-10 of the "world's best-dressed persons," a list headed by Joan Crawford, Bob Hope, and Princess Margaret Rose of England. She earned this recognition, it was reported, "because being the best-dressed hillbilly, Judy dresses with a sense of humor." It was also reported that same week that Judy had 766 fan clubs throughout the United States; and, she passed up a 33-day engagement and high salary to be the star attraction of the Cole Bros. Circus during the summer of 1949 because of the length of the engagement. Annie also made a slight splash when it was announced that the Actors Laboratory in Hollywood would be trying out an original operetta that she wrote.

Ironically, Judy and Chester B. England's Los Angeles divorce was finalized on Valentine's Day of 1949. As of March of 1949 Judy was often seen in the company of a dentist, 36-year-old Dr. Robert Thompson. But on April 1, 1949, Thompson died in a plane crash in the mountains between Los Angeles and Palm Springs, five miles north of Beaumont, California. Judy had originally planned to join Robert on the trip, but was forced to cancel her plans because of an important business deal that came up. "And besides," she later said, "I was nervous about flying in a private plane." The couple had a date that night for a movie. (Reports stated that had he lived, he and Judy would have been on their honeymoon the following month. Yet, a few news items also stated that she was seeing Bob Lowery and Jim Morton at the same time.) She collapsed

The real Judy Canova.

upon hearing the news of Thompson's crash and was placed under a doctor's care. She told Louella Parsons a few days later: "We had no marriage plans because I have just obtained my divorce. But he was the sweetest, most thoughtful friend I have ever had, and perhaps I would have married him."

As of May, 1949 Judy's name was being mentioned as a possible replacement to Doris Day (herself replacing Judy Garland) in the screen version of Irving Berlin's classic *Annie Get Your Gun* (released in 1950). Betty Garrett, Vera-Ellen and Betty Grable were also rumored for the star slot. Sources state that producers Richard Rodgers & Oscar Hammerstein II had been trying for two years to get Judy Canova to tour with the show. MGM had its own ideas, and finally spent $100,000 to borrow Betty Hutton from Paramount for the picture. It was co-star Howard Keel's major screen debut, and took in more than $8 million at the box office.

In December of 1949 Judy did an air show broadcast with special guest William Boyd. The teaming of Judy and Hopalong Cassidy received a fair amount of press and led to rumors of a joint tour, as well as adding more interest in a Canova TV series.

Judy loved radio, but like everyone else in 1950, she knew television was too big to ignore.

Still, as of March 1950, Judy's series was tied for sixth place in the ratings with *People Are Funny*, after *Fibber McGee & Molly, Red Skelton, Grand Ole Opry,* and *Bing Crosby.* (A year later, she was number four, just ahead of Jack Benny, and just behind Red Skelton.) Of the lead-off show to the new season, *Variety* wrote, on October 11, 1950, that the premiere episode was "a half-hour of corn, spottily buttered with songs… makes up the usual format of this Judy Canova airer … Program may have difficulty drawing the sophisticates but for the more earthy dialers it's okay fun. Brand of humor delivered on the show is derived mainly from references to mountain family life, backwoods talk, and mispronunciation and misuse of words." They praised her singing, too, calling her a hard worker.

Branching out further, Judy invaded herself a new medium in early May 1950 when the Judy Canova comic book made its debut from Fox Feature Syndicate. It was to be a bi-monthly edition showcasing the characters on her show.

This was also the month she got back together with Herbert J. Yates, head of Republic Pictures, for a long-term contract which stated she would make two pictures a year, backed by a $500,000 publicity campaign, and Judy touring all "important" cities where her pictures would play. Republic was interested in refashioning two Mabel Normand silent features into vehicles for Judy.

Honeychile (1951) was probably the best title for one of her films since it ties in directly with the plot (a similar idea to *Puddin' Head*): It seems Judy Canova (her own self) wrote the song "Honeychile" which has just

been recorded by a big-time publisher and attributed to famous composer Marvin McKay (John Crawford) due to a mix up in the office. President Al Moore (Walter Catlett) is frantic that he doesn't own the song, so he sends right-hand man Eddie Price (Eddie Foy, Jr.) out to secure the song rights for a hundred bucks. But Judy can't sell it — she's giving it to her man Joe Boyd (Alan Hale, Jr.) as a wedding present. Poor Eddie tries everything (including temporarily breaking up their romance) to get the song, but to no avail. Al himself comes out to offer her $5k and a royalty for the song, providing she'll sign the contract which admits that McKay wrote the song. Judy reluctantly agrees to sign after learning that Joe has bet someone else's money on his winning the local Frontier Day wagon race. The town scorns her for claiming that she wrote a song — there's a different composer named on the record label, after all. But after winning the race and being made guest of honor for Frontier Day, McKay himself is on hand to tell the town the truth and request a rendition of "Honeychile" from the rightful composer.

The film had a good plot, if a little clunky at times, with some able comedy (especially the scene in which Eddie attempts to make love to Judy in the parlor) and several songs, including the toe-tapping title ditty.

It was Judy's first film in five years, and Republic's first use of the new "Trucolor" process, a three-color system by way of Eastman Kodak's Monopack color negative and the new DuPont color print stock. Judy publicly expressed enthusiasm for the process: "If the final results are like the tests, it'll be beautiful." She also had a small financial stake in the film.

She learned to ride a horse for the role, after a few months of concentrated effort. Later, she would ride a horse down Hollywood Blvd. in the Santa Claus Lane parade.

Back at Republic, Judy found another strong role in *The WAC from Walla Walla* (1952), teeming with plenty of fish-out-of-water shenanigans, and, of course, a few more songs to sing: "Lovely," "If Only Dreams Came True," and "Boy, Oh Boy" by Jack Elliott, plus the chorus for all the girls, "Song of the Women's Army Corps" by Harold Spina and Jack Elliott. It was another wartime plot, with more than a touch of hillbilly fuedin'.

The plot: From Bull Run to World War I the Canovas have been war heroes; so it comes as a disappointment to her parents, during one dark and stormy flashback, when Judy is born instead of an expected son. The same night that lightning destroys the town square statue of Canova.

Just before Halloween of 1950 the Los Angeles Junior Chamber of Commerce named Judy "Miss Droopert of 1950" for a traffic safety week that was much publicized in local newspapers. She was chosen as a comic figure to show drivers just how many women are guilty of Droopertisms. (Droopert was a "zany, masculine character who snarls traffic with his unorthodox driving techniques, runs down pedestrians," never signals for turning, and generally makes hell for drivers and pedestrians alike.)

Good riddance, claims Col. Mayfield (Thurston Hall), who was trying to get the thing taken down ("He don't even attract a good grade o' pigeon."). His bitterness comes from the fact that the Mayfields and Canovas have been feuding for generations. Jud "Gramps" Canova II (George Cleveland) keeps trying to rebuild the statue, but Judy always seems to cause it unintentional harm. Years later, just as handsome Lt. Tom Mayfield (Stephen Dunne) is returning as a war hero, a Mayfield statue is about to be erected; the Canovas rush over with their own refurbished relative. Once the fight's started again, Col. Mayfield contends that when a Canova is decorated again, he'll pay for a *new* statue to go up right beside the Mayfield's.

All Judy cares about is seeing Tom again, but so does Doris Vail (June Vincent), the snooty local dress shop owner. Doris tricks Judy into almost joining the WACs, but when Tom makes a fuss over her patriotism, not only does Judy really join, but so does Doris (after hearing that Judy will be assigned to a training facility next door to where Tom's stationed). Poor Judy is tricked a few more times, but kindly WAC Sgt. Kearns (Irene Ryan) makes a note of Judy's attitude and her splendid singing ability and wants to help her as much as possible.

At this point a subplot involving spies is introduced. It seems that Redington (Allen Jenkins) is trying to kidnap Tom for the secret of the new air missile. They don't quite snag him, so they keep an eye on him at the army base until they're finally ready to throw in a fake general who tries to bluff his way into getting some written notes on the missile from Doris and Judy who are now working in the Ordinance Dept. However, this general's name is "Mayfield" and he actually compliments the Canovas, so Judy knows he's a phony. Doris rushes off to alert Tom and the Army while Judy takes off after the baddies, and after a frenzied chase, she finally thwarts all. At a special ceremony in town, not only is Sgt. Judy decorated, but the town finally erects that new & improved Canova statue, seemingly bringing peace to two *very* fussy families.

The script was a punchy bit of fun, with some frothy friction coming from Doris and June. When Judy asks her, "What type shade would you say is best for my complexion?" the vamp answers, "I'd say a window shade." Of course, Allen Jenkins is always a tough guy crowd pleaser, though when he's not getting the job done near the end of the film, his boss criticizes, "The next time I send an idiot, I'll go myself!"

The WAC from Walla Walla was in production from May 12 to early June of 1951. Judy had to return the following month to shoot some additional scenes since filming had been delayed into May because of a viral infection she'd suffered.

Tweeny made her film debut in *WAC* (playing Judy as a little girl), but Judy stated that "I don't want her to like acting too much until she is older." Julieta explains, "I was in three of Mom's movies when I was a kid, and [had] a stint on *The Mickey Mouse Club*, as well as some state fair work with her. But having been raised in the business, it was pretty much what I considered normal: out of the house very early, on the set at a prescribed time making sure you knew your dialogue, and lyrics, if necessary. The singing was weird to me inasmuch as stage work was live, but TV and film was prerecorded so you either lipsync or sing along when you're putting the scene on film. And when you're under 18, due to California Child Labor Laws, you go to school on the set and/or you have a 'social worker/teacher' assigned to you. I really don't remember having been the only kid on any of the film sets except once, and that was pretty boring since it was just like having someone monitor you doing homework."

Oklahoma Annie (1952) began shooting the following month, through all of July and August, with parts of it filmed at the Corriganville Movie Ranch in Simi Valley, California. After this 90-minute film, the Texas Rangers named Judy "Queen of the Cowgirls," a title that was promised to be added to her billing on subsequent films.

Singing "Blow the Whistle" (by Sterling Sherwin and Harry McClintock) to a kid while demonstrating the electric train set he wants, she's given a whole eight cents down as a deposit on the $80+ unit. Yeah, times are tough running her trading post on the edge of the town of Eureka, as she still owes the bank a $600 mortgage on the place. She has *half* of it, which she gives to two old-timer prospector friends to drop off at the bank for her. But stopping for a thirst quencher at the local crooked gambling house, they quickly lose her life's savings at the dishonest roulette wheel. She complains to the hunky new sheriff, Dan Fraser (John Russell), to whom she's taken a shine. Unfortunately, the owner of the Coffin Creek Café, Bull McCready (Grant Withers), also owns Eldridge Haskell (Frank Ferguson), the county supervisor, who tips Bull off that the honest sheriff and Judy are coming over. Instead of a coarse bar/gambling joint they find the bartender (Allen Jenkins) serving fizzy drinks to guys knitting and feeding the kitty (not poker — giving milk to a cat, of course). Judy knows the joint's been tipped off and it irks her courageous blood; her grandmother, after all, was Oklahoma Annie, a former sheriff of the county. (When crooks knew she was comin' for 'em, they'd either reform or hang themselves.)

Dan jokingly tells Judy that *she* can be sheriff when she catches the crook who recently robbed the town's bank — the notorious Curt Walker

(Roy Barcroft). Not surprisingly, Judy lucks into catching him and gets her tin star. She soon embarrasses Dan by calling his car radio to ask what color curtains he wants in the jail, a dumb mistake since just moments later she needs his help to squelch a gunfight that's broken out across the street. It's a ruse to lure Judy away and break Curt out of jail, which also puts Dan out of a job. Rounding up a posse to ride out toward the bogus

Sheriff Judy.

location Haskell gave where he spotted Curt hiding out, Judy overhears a woman telephoning that she'll meet Curt at the Coffin Creek Café that night, and convinces Dan to check it out. Haskell rides along to proposition the sheriff into playing ball with Bull and the boys, and Dan manages to play along after flipping his two-way radio switch up so Judy can hear he's in trouble. She rings the bell to excite all the volunteer firewomen to jump on the two old fire engines and race out to chop the dirty place down once and for all. Judy saves the sheriff who becomes the new county supervisor. Dan's first job: Appoint Judy the new sheriff!

Judy Canova was supposed to have begun the independent feature, "The Hot Heiress," in England the summer following *Oklahoma Annie*, now that her radio series was off for the summer. But because of the "timeliness" of the plot of *A WAC from Walla Walla*, *Wac* was the film rushed into production in April of 1951.

Romance got in the way, as well.

CHAPTER TEN
Rivero

Busy with a booming film career and young Tweeny to supervise, Judy wasn't dating much. Though she *was* seen out a few times, like at the Biltmore Bowl with Dr. Robert Thompson. Then, on September 7, 1950, Louella Parsons announced to her readers that our gal Judy had been the secret bride of wealthy Cuban importer, Philip Rivero, for the past ten weeks. The couple had kept it a secret, it was said, because Judy's 80-year-old mother, Henrietta Canova, had been ill, and the doctor advised against excitement; unfortunately, her health only worsened, and she died of a heart ailment in Burbank's St. Joseph's Hospital on August 30, 1949, without ever having learned the good news.*

Philip and Judy had married in a little town outside Mexico City. They lived together for a time in North Holiday.

And on June 1, 1953, in West Palm Beach, Florida, a little girl — Diana Canova, weighing eight pounds, 14.5 ounces — was born.

"Tweeny" (Julieta), "Fili" (Philip), Judy and Diana, Christmas, 1953.

"When my father and mother met," says Diana, "they met on the *Yankee Clipper* on the way to New York from Havana. Love at first sight. The sad thing is, I don't remember them happy. If you ask my sister, she will be able to shed light on the early days as my dad pretty much raised her from when she was seven or so. I just remember unpleasantness between them.

"My father was always on the phone speaking in rapid fire Cubano and my mother couldn't understand [him], which made her crazy. My father spoke only English to me. Mom couldn't speak Spanish at all and could understand even less. I learned the language later when I was around my Cuban cousins and when I took it in high school.

"When Castro took over and Dad couldn't go home to Cuba, he became obsessed with trying to get his country back and — or helping refugees. It became a big priority. My mother was used to being treated as the *only*

---

*Rivero's father was personal physician to President Batista of Cuba.

priority. It was all she knew. She had been the star of the family since she was 12, and when someone else stole the focus, she didn't handle it well. Also, she had major asthma and was taking a lot of cortisone and prednisone, every day, and my father said it really changed her personality for the worse. That was when they really started having problems and she cut him off.

Fili and Judy.

"My dad never cheated. This I know. He wasn't like all the other Latinos in Hollywood who went out on their wives. His mistress truly was the 'anti-revolution,' and eventually it killed him. He dropped dead on a Friday morning right before my birthday, and he wasn't even sixty.

"My mother was always complaining about the 'goddamn Cubans!' mainly because he put all his effort in that situation which was a war he was never going to win. She saw the futility in it. She knew he was 'pissin' in the wind,' but there was no talking to him. I find it unfortunate that she didn't acknowledge the honor in it. And the passion. Not to mention the heartbreak of a country and homeland lost to all these people. I feel it to this day, which is the major regret I have, in that I would have loved going back with my Dad at some point. I will never know Cuba with him or without him. My mom just didn't get it. I never understood why.

"Who was the 'love of her life?'... I don't know. She was married four times and I really think my dad was the 'lust in her life.'

"My dad was really a fun-loving, passionate Cuban who also had a very hot temper, and one look from him could scare me to death. He wasn't a large or imposing guy, just loud. I didn't have the proper relationship with him that I should have had because they divorced when I was ten. My mother was always sick with asthma and my father was always hollering, and the minute my sister could get the heck out of there, she did.

Judy maybe feeling that Cuban influence.

*Above: Fili Rivero and Judy on their honeymoon in Cannes — touring Europe.
Below: In Barcelona.*

"My father was buried on my eighteenth birthday and, as I get older, I regret not having had him in my life more. I felt I never knew him well enough. He loved me to death, but was stubborn in so many ways. Also very religious. Catholic. Raised by Jesuits in Havana. I was way too sensitive and scared of him to have the kind of fun with him I could have. Cubans are very special people. I love that I have that in me. The passion and zest for life is something I remember about him. He was a musician. That was big with me. That's when we got along well. I just wish that I could have known him while I was an adult. One thing I know he would have hated was that we made fun of the priest on *Soap*. He would not have been into that at all. For that, he would have disowned me.

"I went to Mass every day when I was in boarding school. When I was home, I would go to Mass early Sunday mornings and then go to Protestant services with my mother's family. By the time I was ten years old I'd had it with all the religions. Too many conflicting views. Very confusing for a kid.

"My most vivid memory of my dad is him rolling up his pant legs on Hollywood Boulevard and doing the can-can. And he always smoked Kent cigarettes. I never saw him with a cigar in his mouth. He looked like a Cuban Cary Grant. He really did. I've seen him in pictures at Varadero Beach, and he was kind of fabulous. He was a track star in Cuba. His family belonged to the Havana Yacht club. He had five brothers and they all could sail. My mother called him "Fili," pronounced *filly*. I always thought it so funny that in English his name was Filbert. After a nut. In Spanish he was called Filiberto. *Mas romantico*. He could write very well. He wrote many articles on the revolution. He was so upset with me that I wouldn't date Cuban boys. He thought American boys were 'oafs.'"

CHAPTER ELEVEN

Them Flicks Is Packin' Up

Why in the world Judy Canova (*Judy Canova*) should sport a thick country accent when she grew up in an orphanage full of Northern accents is anybody's guess. But that's what happens in Republic Pictures' *Untamed Heiress* (1954). She's singled out by a couple of crooks, Walter Martin (Taylor Holmes) and Eddie Taylor (Chick Chandler), who are trying to locate the lost daughter of Effie Canova. Old prospector

Untamed Heiress, *1954.*

Cactus Clayton (George Cleveland) has offered them a thousand bucks to locate her so he can give her half of the gold he found in them thar hills; Effie staked him a while back, and he's never forgotten the kindness of that great singer. But to track her down, Martin and Taylor have to con money again out of the none-too-smart gangster Spider Mike Lawrence (Donald Barry) who ultimately takes quite a hankerin' to Ms. Judy. To stop Mike from killing them, the con men let him in on the deal, and with Judy adopted, everyone heads out for Clayton's castle in the desert. Too bad the ol' coot's cracked, or so it seems. But Clayton and Judy take to one another like granddaughter to grandfather, and all she wants is to stay and take care of the old tetched feller. Besides, it seems something's not right with Williams (Hugh Sanders) who says he's looking after Clayton with the aid of two men in white coats. She's right; soon she finds out that the benevolent codger is being held under duress until they can find out where he's hidden his gold. Using the "truth gas" works and, after fighting with Mike and his faithful-yet-dumb helper, Louie (Jack Kruschen), the true villains take off with what they think is the chest of gold. What they don't realize is that, years before, the gold was melted down and painted to resemble a huge ball and chain, to which Mike has already chained Walter Martin.

Tweeny, Judy and Fili.

After an aggressive battle, Williams and his men are subdued and the gold is safe. Judy has asked Clayton to let her adopt him as his grandpa, and he agrees. Still, she has time for a world tour as the "famous daughter of a famous mother," singing as the Nugget City Nightingale, and ends the film with a rousing rendition of "Sugar Daddy."

Untamed Heiress was filmed under the title of "The Hot Heiress" during December 1953 and released by Republic on April 12, 1954. It was delayed a bit by the birth of Diana Canova, and the completion of Judy's previous *Oklahoma Annie*. Some news items state that the original story was to be set in London, redrafted for Boston, and ended up in the Southwest. The screenplay was authored by Judy and Jack Townley, although only Townley received story credit. This was also one of the few times Tweeny appeared on screen.

"I acted from the age of five to about twelve — in a couple of Mom's movies and a couple of episodes of *The Mickey Mouse Club*," Julieta recalls. "When I experienced more rejection than I cared to, I thought the best move was to go into the business world and leave the acting side to community theatre or public speaking. My creative side sort of tends towards writing anyway."

Judy Canova kept going. But there wasn't much time left in the Republic contract.

Filmed in just a few short weeks in August and September of 1954, *Carolina Cannonball* was released on January 28, 1955. The plot reflected the nervous feeling of the time: When the U.S. government's first atomic-powered missile goes missing, three foreign agents (Sig Ruman, Leon Askin, and Jack Kruschen) rush out into the desert after it. The only vehicle that can get them to the (ghost) town of Roaring Gulch is the *Carolina Cannonball*, an old-fashioned, steam-driven streetcar running on railroad tracks. The CC is operated by Judy Canova (Judy Canova) and her nearly deaf grandpa (Andy Clyde). Neither Judy nor Grandpa is aware that the shiny, silver missile is sticking out of the ground nearby, nor do they have a clue that the foreign agents aren't *really* the uranium prospectors they claim to be. When government agent Don Mack (Ross

Elliott) also shows up claiming to be a prospector, it's spy vs. spy until the baddies tell Judy that Don's stolen something from their room. Judy helps subdue Don in a mine by throwing a ton of rocks on him, and urges the handsome man to apologize for his wrongdoing. The foreign agents accept Don's apology instead of sending him to jail so they can coerce information out of him.

Facing page, above: Carolina Cannonball, *1955.*

Meantime, Judy and Grandpa have to fix the CC which almost blew up. Good thing they've found this shiny metal thing sticking out of the ground that they got for a new boiler. And boy, don't that new boiler make top speed! The only drawback is that the scrap metal Judy saved for a bracelet is making all things electric (lights, player piano, pinball machine) pop to life whenever she passes by them. The spies figure it out, too, with the aid of their tracking equipment, and capture Judy so they can run off and locate the bulk of the atomic material. She and Don untie themselves in time to latch onto the CC as Grandpa takes off at break-neck speed. The bad guys hop on and eventually take over the streetcar, but are blown up once the Air Force learns of the threat. It's okay, though, since it looks like the Canovas are going to get a replacement CC, and are once again souped up for the coming atomic age.

This pedestrian comedy had a few things going for it. On the song side, Judy's lovely voice can be heard belting out three original songs by Donald Kahn and Jack Elliott: the title song, "Busy as a Beaver" and the standout ballad, "Wishin' and Waitin'." On the comedy side, all the break-away furniture in the hotel is good for a few laughs. Plus, lead villain Sig Ruman is great at ruining the English language with his "Yoo whom!" and "What kind of place this is?!" Still, with such a small cast, even the many ghost town sets make it a rather cheap-looking film. The score by R. Dale Butts is excellent, however.

Variety had this to say: "the reality of recent times relating to spies, enemy agents, and atomic secrets, hardly makes the subject a laughing matter. In the light of what has happened and the continuing danger, it seems a dis-service to portray these agents as stupid, left-footed nincompoops."

Judy's last Republic picture fared better, at least financially, and as a film.

The terribly misnamed *Lay That Rifle Down* (1955) did pack a lot of entertainment in 71-minutes, including three more charming Elliott/Kahn songs for Judy. Half a Cinderella tale, the plot involved Judy (under her own name, of course) working like a slave for her unappreciative Aunt Sarah Greeb (Jacqueline deWit) and her daughter (Jil Jarmyn) at the Greebville Hotel. She's a loyal-but-lonely gal who wants to improve herself by taking a correspondence charm school course. When she tries to stop the staff from laughing at the idea, she tells them that the latest missive is actually a letter from her feller, Poindexter March III.

Cajoled into meeting him at the bus station, she simply latches onto the first attractive male who steps off the bus. To her delight, Nick Stokes (Robert Lowery) goes along with the gag, but only because he knows an honest rube when he sees one. He and his partner (Robert Burton) have a con worked out to bilk the local bank out of $25,000, using the farm ranch Judy's parents left her as bait. Nick's partner pretends to be a gen-eral on a secret mission to buy that spot of land for a new and vital war plant. The banker (Richard Deacon) merges his greed with Aunt Sar-ah's to try get the farm for a song; but Nick makes Judy promise that she won't sing for less than $25k, at which point he'll have her sign the check over to him. Too bad for the bogus general that Nick has pangs of guilt and backs out on the deal. The "general" conks him on the head, hijacks the swag, and a chase ensues to find the varmint. He escapes to the bank and Judy shoots him with her old shotgun as he's driving away. The car explodes. In the nick of time, Judy gets her farm back from the disgusted banker, and the *real* government comes along just then to offer her $100,000 for the property.

Once again, there are a few highlights: "The Continental Correspondence Charm School" is a good singing showcase for Judy. But perhaps most interesting is the precocious presence of Tweeny Canova as Tweeny Greeb.

In an article about Hollywood stars preferring that their offspring not follow in their footsteps, Judy was quoted as saying, "If my daughter

decides she wants to go into show business it will be all right with me. And if being Judy Canova's daughter will be of any help to her, I'll be tickled to death. The decision is up to my daughter. As I see it, my job is to give her a chance to find and express herself."

Julieta Canova states, "I don't really have any specific memories about any of the films. From what I *do* remember, there seemed to be a compatibility with the cast and crew, and the director was never difficult. But I was required to spend time in school while on the set, so I wasn't actually around unless they needed me for a scene. I didn't, however, need a 'social worker' to be there since my mom was always on set."

Though her film career was winding down, Judy appeared on several top TV shows of the 1950s. On *The Mickey Mouse Club* she and Tweeny are given guest star status and dominate most of the show until the cartoon shows up. After Judy is introduced, Tweeny finds herself alone in the dressing room where she struts while changing many hats, singing "With the Proper Hat." When Judy returns and puts on her "yodeling clothes," mother and daughter sing a duet. After the commercial, Judy calls a square dance by way of "The Doggy Danced All Night." The songs of the show were credited to several, including Judy and Anne Canova.

"*The Mickey Mouse Club* was a very good experience," says Julieta. "Despite what some people say about Mr. Disney, he was gracious to us, although we only really saw him twice. The Mouseketeers that I went to the on-set supervised 'school' with, during the time we worked, were all nice, but not anything of lasting friendships. I didn't see any temper tantrums; there were no ego trips and only *one* stage mother (but I can't remember whose mom it was). They all knew their lines, hit their marks and moved on with it. One of the guys (Bobby Burgess) went on to a long career working on *The Lawrence Welk Show*, and I do remember him as being bright and a pretty down-to-earth kid — as far as kids raised in the entertainment field can be. And of course there was Annette Funicello, but I don't even remember her being around.

"That's about it. Except they don't let you keep the mouse ears — they were just props."

In 1958 Judy had one of her best showcases on *Make Room for Daddy*, starring Danny Thomas. Judy is Elsie Hoople, wife of the owner of the diner where Danny (Thomas) finds himself temporarily stranded and without a singer for his show. Judy belts one out for Danny, but has to resist his offer to come to the New York nightclub because of the estrangement between the Hooples. He seems to love his prize pig more than her, which finally gives her the courage to take her $13 in egg money and hop a bus to follow Danny for that chance in his show. Staying with them and admiring their amazing view of the brightly lit Great White Way, Judy keenly comments that "you'd think the last one to go home would turn 'em off." The nightclub audience is ecstatic with her deadpan yodeling, as she dashes between pop and operatic timber. After a heartfelt "I Don't Know Why I Love You Like I Do" aimed at her husband, Judy has backstage dreams of having a star's life: fur that still has the head and tail on it, going to Hollywood to get herself a pool in the shape of "a sweet patater." But in walks her husband, who finally tells her what he never could before — *he needs her*. That's the greatest prize of all.

Even with some top shows behind her, it was difficult to get much interest in her own TV pilot of *The Judy Canova Show* that would show her life on the road as a traveling carnival entertainer. The first episode was shot in 1958, but did not land enough sponsor interest to even air over a network.

She tried again the next year, perhaps this time connecting to her high-profile *Daddy* appearance, since this new situation comedy would show Judy as the owner of a diner in the Ozarks. Another unaired pilot was made, but it also failed to click.

Our gal Judy in one o' them '60s hair-don'ts!

Luckily the new decade saw Judy back on the big screen as part of the all-star telling of *The Adventures of Huckleberry Finn* (1960), about the timely relationship of Huck (Eddie Hodges) and his slave-friend, Jim (Archie Moore). Escaping a wicked father, Huck fakes his own death, but when Jim is hunted for the crime, the two of them set off on a found raft together. Their adventures mostly involve evading the posse after Jim and

February, 1960.

the evil revenge of The King (Tony Randall) and his sidekick, The Duke (Mickey Shaughnessy) after Huck publicly tells the truth regarding one of their many cons.

Down the Mississippi River of 1851, the duo come in contact with many celebrities in cameos, including Buster Keaton as a second-string lion tamer, Andy Devine as a bottom-rung circus owner, Sterling Holloway as a barber, and, near the end of the picture, Judy Canova as the sheriff's wife. When Jim is finally captured, Huck ventures into the sheriff's house to get the key to unchain his friend from the barn. To avoid suspicion, Huck dresses as a girl, but Huck quickly gives himself away by looking at the hanging keys, looking for the stitch Judy "lost" while at her needlework, and threading the needle wrong. "Trying to hornswoggle me!" she shouts. He and Jim still escape, though they are ultimately caught. But Huck brilliantly turns the tables on The King so that *he* goes to jail and the two friends go free.

There wasn't much for Judy to do in the film, but it must have been good to see her on the big screen again, in Technicolor, in a major motion picture.

Nineteen-sixty *was* a good year, one which gave Judy one of her most rewarding TV roles. The May 29, 1960 episode of *Alfred Hitchcock Presents* ("Party Line") has Helen Parch (Canova) tying up a party line with gossip when a man pleads for her to get off the phone so he can call for an ambulance. She denies his request and his wife dies as a result. Months later, the man is sentenced to prison for a murder and now, two years from the day that she caused the death of his wife, he breaks out of prison. When Helen discovers that he is outside the house seeking vengeance, she attempts to phone the sheriff's department for help — only to fall victim to her own turnabout, since two gossipy women will not get off the party line.

According to Martin Grams, Jr., co-author of *The Alfred Hitchcock Presents Companion*, "This was Hilton A. Green's only episode of the series that he directed. He was an assistant director for the series, but took command with this one. 'I didn't get to choose which story to do,' he recalled, 'I was just assigned to it and I did it. Judy Canova was the star and I think she was wonderful.' Author Henry Slesar, whose story was adapted for the episode, recalled how he saw his story characters brought to life by people like Claude Rains and Judy Canova."

She kept trying for TV stardom, but there were new executives making the decisions these days. On September 5, 1967 she was seen in NBC's pilot for *Li'l Abner*, based on the popular Al Capp comic strip. Judy was her regular hick self as kindly Mammy Yokum, lookin' out for the welfare of the beautiful Daisy Mae (Jeannine Riley), who has bewitched Senator Henry Cabbage Cod (Robert Reed) with her ravishing nature.

Once again, this proposed series never made it beyond the first episode.

Another unsuccessful pilot, this time for ABC, involved a retelling of the old Romeo & Juliet/Hatfields & McCoys story. This time it was "The Murdocks and the McClays" episode on September 2, 1970 for the proposed *Comedy Preview*. Judy was Ida Murdock, aided by Dub Taylor, Kathy Davis, Noah Beery, Jr., and others.

Maybe it was time for a little retirement.

CHAPTER TWELVE

Nearin'the End

The 1970s were uneventful, except for failing health. In 1968 Judy had spent 46 days in the hospital for treatment of a respiratory ailment. She never fully recovered. It slowed down her career considerably, though she still found the energy for the odd TV show when one was offered to her.

"Mom was not a slapstick queen around the house," says Diana. "Her personality was totally normal. It was all business. Once in a while she

Older, and — wiser?

would get a kick out of something and she did love to laugh, but she wasn't a lighthearted gal *at all*. At least not when I knew her. She was usually very sick and that really colored her personality, as you can imagine.

"She was no hillbilly and it really irked her that people thought of her as one. She always used to say how someone — can't remember, maybe Walter Winchell? — said that 'Judy Canova was about as hillbilly as the

Above: Christmas, 1971. Below: June, 1972.

Duchess of Windsor.' She was very proud of that statement and repeated it a lot."

It may well have been the fact that she was still being typecast (even in her advancing years) that caused fewer roles to be offered to her. The western craze had peaked, with more extreme films like *The Godfather* and *The Exorcist* coloring Hollywood's mainstream features into something too extreme and serious for the likes of a Judy Canova.

Still, there were a few roles that came around. In 1972 she appeared in the touring company of *No, No, Nanette* with Virginia Mayo, Dennis Day, Sandra Deel and Jerry Antes.

There was also the nothing role as backseat mom in *Cannonball!* (1976). The precursor to Burt Reynolds' highly successful *Cannonball Run* by just five years, the film gave equal time to a group of long-distance drivers who are speeding from Los Angeles to New York to claim the $100,000 prize and win a spot as a driver for the secretive company sponsoring the illegal contest. Evading cops and smashing up the competition is the name of the game in what writer/director Paul Bartel called a comedy. The showdown between hero/star David Carridine (Cannonball, the greatest underground driver in the world) and bad guy Bill McKinney was the main focus of the feature, ending in Bill's crash-and-burn atop an incomplete bridge. It had its moments, but was obviously a cheaply made knockoff of the cult classic, *Death Race 2000* (1975).

Judy was probably the only character in the film who was completely unnecessary, with few lines except complaining to manic driver Cade Redman (McKinney) when he shouts at her son, untalented guitarist Zippo Friedman (Archie Hahn). Why the mother and son are in the car is hard to say, but Zippo keeps busy by singing and playing his guitar into a microphone which is broadcasting his unbelievable songs to various radio stations. Sharman Capri (Judy) merely smiles and nods no matter what sounds the guy makes, while Cade merely grips the steering wheel tighter, finally chucking the instrument out the window. Luckily, he also tosses the odd couple out of the car before driving to his fiery doom.

Diana muses, "She did *Cannonball!* I expect because there was nothing else [being offered]. Maybe she did it for the SAG insurance. Maybe because they asked her to. She chanted in those days, so maybe she

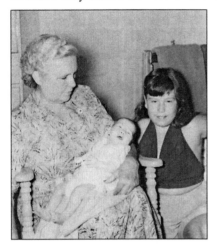

Right: Gogga, baby Diana, and Tweeny. Left: D&T, sisters forever.

thought the offer was a result of that. The Buddhist chant. She found that kind of meditation good for awhile.

"Mom had every 'positive thinking' and 'self-meditation' book there was. Once in awhile she'd go to a Catholic Church and light a candle. She was big on prayer, but oddly, [she was] never a 'religious' person. She was just searching for a way to be happy, because she was not ever happy.

"She had major problems with alcohol during the seventies. The last fifteen years of her life were spent drinking. I made a decision early on that I would not let the business chew me up and spit me out like they did her. She must have been really fun as a kid. She was goofy and funny, and then she was successful and a star who everyone loved, and I know she thought it would stay that way, and when it didn't, she didn't look to me and go, 'Wow, well, I'll put my energy into Diana, (my sister was already out of the house by that point) and have a good life without being a star.' She didn't, or couldn't, so it was a struggle. Plus, being sick all the time from emphysema was very tough for her. Just trying to breathe was a struggle.

"I remember that most of the time when I was a kid, I would come home from school to find her in bed with her bed jacket on and her hair in a net, coughing away. *Or* being carted away once again to the hospital because she had had an especially bad day. It was not unusual to see the ambulance in the driveway.

"She was described by one of the fellows that married into the family as 'tough.' Not because she was a 'slap a smile on your face and seize the day' kind of tough, either. 'Hard as nails' kind of tough."

Julieta adds, "Mom really started drinking when her career slowed

Top: Tweeny, little Diana, and Judy roaming the estate. Bottom left: Judy and Diana on the Canova estate. Bottom right: Diana just can't believe it.

down in the seventies. But I do know that it was the fashion in the fifties to have that evening martini. When she met my stepfather, they tried different daiquiri recipes in Key West, Havana and New York. He made really good daiquiris."

Diana Canova held the family spotlight for a while when she was featured on the hit TV series, *Soap*, which boasted one of the greatest TV casts in history (Billy Crystal, Richard Mulligan, Katherine Helmond, Ted Wass, Robert Guillaume, and many other famous faces).

"I was born with the bug," says Diana. "There was never a moment of my life that I considered not being in the business. It was all I ever knew. It was also expected. It was what we understood. …It was just …what we did.

"I know Mom didn't care for *Soap*. She was not happy about my character marrying the priest. She wasn't even Catholic! And yes, she was a bit jealous when I started getting big. However, when I told her she was going to have a grandchild — she was in the hospital with cancer at the time — her response was, 'Well, that's gonna knock the hell out of your career.' I guess that's what she thought had happened to *her* career. She was wrong, though. What happened to her career was that the business had changed by the time she had me. It eventually happens to everybody. Look at what happened to Lucille Ball. The audience wants something new and different which trickles down to the agent not being able to book the artist after awhile. The style of comedy changed that the public was into. Her kind of B-movies was considered 'camp,' and no longer fresh and new.

"My boys Jordi and Matt are Mom's only grandchildren and her only descendants. Matt went to a film festival a couple of years ago where they showed her old films. He turned to me at some point and said, 'Now I know where I get it from. Now I know why I do what I do.' He has always had a rubber body and a crazy sense of humor and is a natural, fearless performer who is full of joy when he's on stage. He gets it from the Cuban side as well, but as he watched my mom it became very clear to him what is in his genes.

"I am happy to report that I came out of my childhood pretty normal and I will attribute it to my mother. I'd like to attribute it to my dad, but he just wasn't there. Good or bad, Mom was an alcoholic, and she smoked too much and she died of lung cancer. She was just not happy. That's the story."

One year before *Soap* ended, Diana left to star in her own series, *I'm a Big Girl Now*, with Danny Thomas, devised by *Soap* creator Susan Harris. It concerned the recently jilted Ben (Thomas), a dentist, who moves in with his daughter (Diana) after his wife of 35 years runs off with his business partner. Robert MacKenzie's review in *TV Guide* stated "though Thomas has the funniest lines, this is Canova's show. She has warmth and a good smile and soft contours, but enough effervescence to give the character some sizzle."

Diana continued acting until 2005, appearing as a guest on such hit series as *Hotel*, *St. Elsewhere*, *Trapper John, M.D.*, and *Murder, She Wrote*.

It was more than the acting bug that the youngster caught from the old trouper. Diana explains, "Mom's speaking voice was very low with a bit of a drawl and when she wanted to make you laugh she would put on

The cast of I'm a Big Girl Now. *Front, left to right: Danny Thomas, Rori King, Diana Canova. Rear, left to right: Sheree North, Michael Durrell, Deborah Baltzell, Martin Short.*

her little hillbilly voice. I have to say that's one thing I inherited from her. And now my sons have taken it on as well.

"Plus, I've been singing all my life and actually started teaching when I was eighteen! I was supposed to be an opera singer but nobody had a sense of humor so I went into musical theater. Mom *could* have been an opera singer because she had a four-octave range. She studied with Nelson Eddy's teacher. She could sing the bell song from *Lakme* and a few other arias but she never pursued it because comedy was really her thing. I still teach mainly because I love it, and I'm good at it. I have a couple of students who have made their Broadway debut before the age of eighteen, which has been a big thrill for me."

Diana and Judy appeared only one time together, on *Dinah!*, Dinah Shore's daytime television talk show, for a 1978 special on mothers and daughters in the entertainment biz. When asked to describe her daughter in one word, Judy smiled and said, "Fantastic." Diana showed off her beautifully smooth voice singing, for the first time on television, a duet with Judy — one of her big hits, "The Warbash Cannonball." Judy herself proved she still had the range and the guts. Diana then went on to sing a lovely ballad that she and husband-at-the-time Geoff Levin wrote together.

"As far as an album deal," says Diana, "I had a singles deal with Twentieth Records right before they turned it into a parking lot. My mom and I sang around the house. The Dinah appearance was the one and only time I performed with her in public."

Julieta enjoyed the celebrity scene for a time, too, although she admits, "Chris [Costello, daughter of Lou] was really the only celebrity kid I hung out with — and that was in our late teens/early twenties. I went to school with other celebrity kids (Max Factor, Jr., Glenn Ford's son, parties at John Wayne's daughter's place), but they were just other kids/teens. Growing up in that environment is normal — it's exactly the same as growing up in a middle-class home in the middle of the country — your friends are your friends for the same reasons anyone picks friends. But making the transitions from school to school and having people find out you're the child of a celebrity is difficult, only because it's normal to have Ernest Borgnine and Rory Calhoun and Bob Lowery come over for dinner, but it's not normal for *them* [your classmates]. So other kids think you're showing off, name dropping — but … it's really all you know …"

Sick as she was, one thing Judy Canova could always turn to in times of need, or "need to know," was fortune telling. Even as early as the early 1930s Judy was interested in the subject. She had consulted Dr. M. De Marr, astrologer on East 73rd St. in New York City. She was also interested in handwriting analysis, and the great Muriel Stafford once examined her personality via her cursive in a February 24, 1946 article in the *New York Mirror*, in which Stafford stated, "Sincerity is the keynote of Judy's writing. Her baseline (that invisible line on which we write) is steady and straight. Letters are small-sized, clear-cut, evenly spaced, and slanted lightly to the right. Charm is shown in many ways too, including amiable rounded letter-tops with a U-shaped *n* in the signature and a slight dwindling of words."

"Even our mammy and maid, Alma Lacy," says Julieta, "allegedly had psychic powers. She was probably just a good judge of character and situation and candid enough not to edit some of what she saw.

"Point blank, I think Mom was more gullible than she was a 'believer.' She pretty much belonged to the Religion of the Month Club — whatever was in fashion from Catholicism to chanting Buddhism. But I know that she (pardon the expression) pissed away more money on psychics than on anything else. She had a penchant for aligning herself with individuals who were not always the most honest, but they made her feel like she was extraordinarily special, so she'd not allow any negative comments about them. And since the whole family liked to dabble in gambling (with the great poker players and periodic trips to Vegas), but not as high rollers, I think maybe the attraction of the psychics was similar to that.

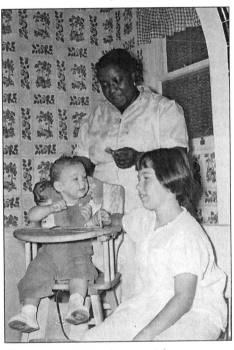

Alma Lacy with the Canova girls.

"Mom was friends with the actor Robert Lowery. He was married to actress Jean Parker (among others), and was always a good guy. His son, Robert Jr., is a little older than my sister but around that same five-year 'generation,' so the families hung out part of the time. Anyway, Robert Lowery's mother was a woman named Nancy Hanks — a self-proclaimed card reader and psychic. So Nancy became one of Mom's best friends. And she'd do 'readings' for her. From where I sat, it was a way to control Mom and get anything she could from her. Nancy would warn her about people and tell Mom not to get too close to them — and as I got older, it was apparent these people were ones who didn't believe a word Nancy said.

"For example, one evening we were sitting in the den — my mom, my sister, Nancy Hanks, and three friends of mine. Nancy proclaimed, 'One of you girls is going to be very, very successful and very, very rich.' Not bad odds in Hollywood when you're sitting in a celebrity's house and two of the girls are her daughters and one of the others in the room is one of Lou Costello's daughters. Unfortunately, Nancy must not have been that good a psychic because Bob Lowery called her one day telling her he didn't feel too well, and he died of a heart attack while on the phone with her. She didn't see it coming.

"Mother also had an African-American friend named Ruth Turner who was another reader. Maybe she had a higher degree of accuracy than Nancy — she was certainly a bit better educated. Highly religious and always did things in the name of The Lord, so crossing her palm with silver was not foremost in her mind. How accurate she was — who knows?

"Smoking and psychics were not her biggest weaknesses. My cousin said, 'Addiction doesn't run in the Canova family, it gallops.' Mom had her bouts with vodka and wine at various times and *those* were her weaknesses. The infamous family poker games-turned-fights were generally because at least two of the siblings and/or their spouses were rip-roaring drunk. As a matter of fact, it was no big deal in those days to serve mini-drinks to the kids.

"I recall one Christmas family dinner where Mom made a very good but very potent champagne punch. My cousin Floretta and I, probably 13 at the time, imbibed enough to get staggery and silly — but the adults were three sheets to the wind and didn't even realize how we'd been affected.

"Mom didn't do pills, [but she] loved ice cream — especially peach ice cream — and she had a hateful little Chihuahua that someone had told her would 'absorb her asthma' for her. The little furball just went around biting ankles and fingers. She named him Tiger.

"The only sport she really liked was as a spectator and that was horser-acing. We'd all pile in the car and drive down to Caliente Race Track in Tijuana a couple of times a year. I was way too young to bet, but they'd let me pick horses and my stepfather would do the betting.

"Mom didn't own any race horses. She was just part of that crowd that would frequent the tracks — they'd socialize there while betting on the nags. She did own a couple of horses during her western B-movie days. The main one was named Penny and she sold it to Rex Allen when Mom stopped making westerns. But she was pretty much afraid of them. She used a handler named Helen to board and train the horses.

"There was a man from Florida who had been friends with Mom and the family in the 'old days.' His name was Lou Wolfson. I believe he made

The Canova Handicap, October 22, 1936 at Arlington Park.

his bucks in scrap metal. Anyway, he owned race horses and named one after Mom — but I don't think it ever ran. I believe that if one names a race horse after a real person that permission is required.

"Speaking of activities, she didn't swim well because she'd been thrown in as a child and she hated to get her face under water. There was a scene she had to do in one of her movies where she and either Eddy Foy, Jr. or Jerry Colonna had to come up from under water and look at each other. She told me they had to do the scene at least 20 times because of her phobia/fear. And she was known as 'the one-take gal'!

"But getting back to fortune telling, my sister and I have each had our cards read/fortunes told at least once, but we don't rely on anything they say — maybe because they're not accurate. I can't think of anyone else in the family who had anything to do with them.

"Mom was also good friends with The Amazing Criswell and his group of friends. Cris was the TV Psychic with the meringue hairdo who was in some Ed Wood movies [including the infamous *Plan 9 From Outer Space*]. Good guy, but just like Jean Dixon and the rest, we probably could make guesses with just as [much] accuracy as them. Cris and his gang appeared to be in it more for the fun and star power aspect than anything else.

"The only [psychic] with any credibility was Peter Hurkos. He came to our house in Hollywood when my mom and stepfather were still married. He didn't so much *predict* the future as he [gave] sensible advice. *But* it was spooky the way he knew things that had never been published and not talked about in *Variety* or *Hollywood Reporter*. He even said to my mom, 'You were very close, almost too close, to your mother. I see her in a rose garden standing like this (and he posed).' There is a picture of our grandmother in that *exact* pose. He couldn't have known it, [since] most of the time it wasn't in plain sight and it had never been published.

"I wound up going into mortgage finance, and in Mom's last two years, I helped her with bills and paperwork, things of that nature. But I never advised her on finances because when I did earlier on, she would do the *opposite* of what I advised. Or she'd consult a psychic, or 'fortch' as she referred to tarot readers and psychics.

"So she wound up getting scammed by a couple of 'business managers.' While she didn't lose everything like some celebrities and athletes, she did lose money and suffered from what we now call 'bag lady syndrome.' That's unmarried women who are aging and scared to death of winding up with nothing but a shopping cart full of raggedy things. I suffer from it myself at times — makes no difference if you have IRAs, 401Ks, stocks, investments or property — if one is unattached, regardless of other family relationships, it's not hard to envision winding up solo in the twilight.

"Another piece of Mom's personality was the fact that she, like most of us, hated being wrong on anything. So if either my sister or I wound up giving her accurate advice, she'd only let the other one know that the information was right. She'd compliment us behind our backs — lauding our accomplishments and abilities to others, but not to our faces for fear we'd grow a big head.

Left to right: Elliot, Diana, Julieta, and Judy at a 1981-82 tribute to Judy.

"Like a lot of women in her time, Mom showed her defiant independence by taking up smoking and having the occasional vodka martini, or glass of wine or daiquiri. What the hell — she was single (had her résumé out for another husband), the bread winner, and a celebrity. She had her stars on the Hollywood Walk of Fame [one for Film at 6821 Hollywood Boulevard, and one for Radio at 6777 Hollywood Boulevard] by virtue of her being a celebrity — now you can just pay for them."

Although she had been chronically ill for many years, Judy's health issues became life threatening in 1983, when she was diagnosed with cancer. As Diana recalls, "I had been living at the house with her when she came home from [having] the biopsy at the hospital; I was in the process of moving back to my house in North Hollywood. A friend of hers came to stay with her when I was working and not there — she even helped me move out. ... So I wasn't there full time, but a lot of it. My sister was there when I wasn't, and our Aunt Anna (Mom's sister) lived in the guest house behind Mom's house.

"Mom went through the stages that doctors describe: denial, anger, acceptance... and I think part of her was angry because none of her 'psychics' had indicated she should stop smoking.

Judy watches Anne play somewhere or other.

"My sister was there when the rep from the American Cancer Society support team visited her at the house and said something about the cancer having spread to her liver. You'll have to ask my sister for that piece [of information] because I wasn't there, but she said that Mom got that look of shock and realization that this was the final chapter, and she had no control over it. That's probably why Diana and I have no respect or love for the physician Mom put so much faith in — he never told her it had spread. So to say that Mom was brave was not totally accurate, but not wrong either.

"She underwent radiation for the lung cancer, even though she knew it was the worst kind (I think it was called 'oat cell'), and she braved it through that treatment. She went through one or two courses, and that took its toll, burning her skin, making red burns plus the marks they made to get the correct location for the radiation. It made her feel like crap. She stopped thriving and pretty much stayed at home.

"You have to know that generation from the South to understand it — *there is never anything wrong*. I don't understand it, even though I was raised with it. It even infected my cousin — Anne's daughter, Juliana — and her younger son (still does). You can talk about the neighbors having their cars repo'd, their husbands' mistresses, their kids' arrests and the holes in their underwear hanging on the clothesline, but *there is never anything wrong* with our own family. And if you admit anything is 'off,' you only do it in a whisper.

"So, some of the people who had been in Mom's life every day knew she was ill, but not what it was nor the severity. She kept that Southern curtain up until the very end.

"But the bond — I think I described it earlier — between my mom and her sister Anne was such that Mom didn't tell her how sick she was because Mom didn't want her upset — and Anne lived in our guest house!

"It got to the point that they'd call each other on the phone instead of walking 250 steps from house to house.

"Mom took a turn for the worse in mid-August and was hospitalized. Not only did she have cancer, but she had been an asthmatic for many years, so her lung capacity was deteriorating and she needed breathing treatments and respiratory therapy to keep going.

"My sister and I were both at her bedside. She'd been hospitalized for a couple of days. She refused chemo probably because she knew there really was no cure for the form of lung cancer she had *or* the liver cancer. Plus — who the hell wants to go bald? Certainly not Mom — she had a great head of hair.

"So she told the doctor to 'let me go,' i.e. *do not resuscitate*."

"I remember the doctor was so upset when he had to tell me she was sick," Diana said, recalling her last days with her mother. "He was furious that she had been smoking for twenty-five years. She had had asthma, and emphysema, and kept buying those Kents. He was also very nervous about telling her she had cancer because he knew she wouldn't take it well. Who would? Her response when the oncologist came into her room was, 'Oh, no, you don't. You're not bringing *me* any coffin.' She only lived for several months after that.

"The day before she died, her doctor came in to see her. He sat on the edge of her bed with a smile and was full of energy and positive things to say. She was on a lot of morphine. He told her about her electrolytes, etc., and was very cheery. Then the two of us went out in the hall, and he leaned against the wall and started to cry. He said, 'You know, everybody thinks doctors are cold and unfeeling, but we are not.' He could not help her. He knew she was dying and he had been her friend and physician for so many years that this was obviously hard on him. He was frustrated, too. Smoking. 'Nuff said.

"The night before she died she looked at me and said, 'You know it's over for me.' I told her I realized that and I asked her if she was okay with it all. She just had this look of resignation on her face. The two of us were alone at that point and she started talking to her mother who I guess was waiting for her. I know the experts say it's just the brain dying, but she did live to the next day and was lucid till practically her last breath, so... I sang 'Go to Sleepy, Little Baby' to her as she went to sleep.

"The next day my sister and I went to her room and hung out. We went to the cafeteria to get a bite to eat and as we were leaving, Mom said, 'Where ya going?' as she had said to me every day of my childhood when I left the house. I told her I was gonna get something to eat and we would be right back. When we did about a half hour later, she was breathing strangely and her eyes were seeing nothing. I took her hand and looked right in her face, and she took her last breath."

Juliette "Judy" Canova died of cancer at age 69 (reported in some papers as 66) in Hollywood Presbyterian Hospital at 4:50 p.m. Friday, August 5, 1983. She left the bulk of her nearly half a million dollar estate to her daughters, which included money, government bonds and Treasury bills; plus her last residence, on Crescent Heights Blvd. in Los Angeles, as well as property in Jupiter Island and Steinhatchee, Florida (20 acres). She bequeathed her sister Anne $5,000 in cash, "my automobile, any clothes of mine she wants, my TV and radio. To my beloved brother Leon, $1,000 in cash to be administered by my daughters because I know I can trust them never to see him in want.

"I leave my beloved daughters my love and admiration because I am proud of them as fine human beings."

Services were held on August 10th at 11a.m. at the Church of the Recessional in Forest Lawn Memorial Park, Glendale. According to her wishes, her body was cremated and interred at Forest Lawn. Her ashes were placed in an urn and placed in the Court of David, Garden of Memory, Columbarium of Everlasting Light, Niche G-706. A memorial tablet there bears the inscription:

Judy Canova
1913 – 1983
Love and Laughter

Judy's Writings

Judy Canova Fulfills
a Lifetime Ambition

(From Hollywood Nite Life, *December 14, 1945. Most certainly written by the studio PR department, but an interesting take on Judy's screen persona.)*

Ever since I was a youngster in Jacksonville, Florida, I wanted to be a movie star. And ever since I've been a movie star, I've wanted to be a columnist so that I could air a few grudges. Now that I've got the chance, however, I can't recall which people I was going to blast!

The same thing happened when the war ended. I had been keeping a mental list of all the storekeepers I wasn't going to do business with after the war — and now I can't remember who they were. A Canova, I guess, resembles an elephant only in one respect: whenever she travels she carries a trunk with her.

It is very funny to think that the post-war era we've all been waiting for is finally here. Frankly, Hollywood doesn't seem much different than it did before. So far, I haven't seen a single person with a walkie-talkie phone, a prefabricated house, or a dress made of non-shrinkable aluminum. The only sign that the post-war period is here is that waitresses no longer ask, "Don't you know there's a war on?" But they still don't look happy to see you. I guess peace just has to grow on people.

In the past three months Hollywood Nite Life has invited "guest stars" to do a column. I think it is a very noble gesture, seeing as how most of the guests, including myself, ought to start the column with a warning like, "If you think I can't write, you ought to hear how I can't play the violin." It reminds me of the story of the woman who wrote a eulogy honoring the great composer, Edward MacDowell. When it was submitted to a publisher, he returned it with this note: "After looking over your composition, I can only say it would have been better if the situation was reversed and MacDowell had written a eulogy about you."

In reading many guest columns, I find that almost all the stars love Hollywood and everybody in it very much. Their accounts of Cinema City bliss somehow bring to mind Mark Twain's visit to a séance. He asked the spirits what they talked about up above and the reply was: "Oh, about our friends back on earth."

Twain pondered this for a moment and then asked: "When all your friends are finally up there with you, what will you talk about?" Of course, the spirit did not answer this, seeing as how spirits will not answer frivolous questions.

Though I've been in Hollywood several years now, I still don't understand it. I can remember back in the days of my youthful movie-going when film queens were a special kind of being who breathed only rarified air and lived more luxuriously than the Pharaohs of old. If they were married no one knew much, if anything, about it.

Today, it's all different. When a movie star gets married her public knows about it before the groom. And they even raise families and let their fans know all about which book they are following in training their offspring. Being a mother myself (her name is Juliette and she is in the year-old stage), I approve of this. In fact, if the "rarefied air" theory about movie actresses had lasted, I wouldn't have — since the only thing rare that just naturally takes to me is a steak!

Turn on the Switch

(Syndicated newspaper article, July 25, 1947)

Things sure do change fast when you ain't watching close. Why, it seems like only yestiddy when, down in my old hill country, electricity was the sparks that flew when a gal brushed her hair real hard. And now, I see by the papers, Americans use up five billion kilowatt hours of the stuff in one week, as much as we used in the whole war year of 1917. (That's since they got to making enough electric irons and toasters and washing machines to sell 'em in stores instead of just giving 'em away on radio programs.)

When you think over what that means, it's enough to make you go grubbing for the old hand saws and spinning wheels that grampa and granny learned how to use because they darn well had to do things for theirselves. Today, a feller could get through a whole day without doing nothing more complicated than pushing buttons and connecting switches.

The buzzer on your electric alarm clock wakes you up, and makes sure you stay awake because it won't stop buzzing till you turn it off. You don't have to bring in firewood and build a fire to keep warm; you just plug in an electric stove in the bathroom while you dress. Instead of stropping his razor, and getting some good healthy exercise, a man only needs the muscle it takes to plug in his electric razor. I hear tell someone's even invented a contraption that brushes your teeth electrically.

You don't need to stand over a hot stove to cook your coffee, toast and eggs. You sit down at a table, and plug 'em in. Instead of hunting up eggs in the henhouse, cutting a slab of bacon in the smokehouse and squeezing oranges for juice, you take them out of the refrigerator in neat packages.

You don't even have to strain your eyes to read the newspaper, and your fingers to turn the pages. You can switch on the radio and get the news already read and digested for you.

Nobody applies elbow grease to a broom; they hitch up the vacuum cleaner. And where it used to take all week for a woman to catch up with the little household matters like washing and ironing and baking, a mite of them kilowatt-hours do the whole job for her now. She tosses the laundry into a washer and waits for it to come out washed, rinsed and half-dried. Then she plugs in an iron and ironer to do most of the finishing. An electric mixer beats up her cakes for her, and the only thing that gets dishpan hands is the electric dish washer.

A man sits at his desk and pushes buttons. One button gets him a telephone line, another brings his secretary a-running, another opens a loudspeaker system so he can talk to all his hired hands at once, and he can have a whole extra flock of buttons to call each and every guy that works for him. When he wants to dictate a letter, he pushes another button and tells it to a record. 'Course, it ain't much fun holding a Dictaphone machine on your lap, but then you can't have everything.

If a farmer wants his hens to lay eggs, he switches on a lot of electric lights and starts the radio to going real loud. At milking time, he just leads Bossy to the milking machine, hitches her up, and goes on about his business. (Say, what do you suppose Bossy thinks about her new deal?)

But the modern man that takes the prize for my money is a Hollywood producer I heard about. Seems he hated to get up in the morning, but figured that if there wasn't no way of getting out of it, it'd be right nice to wake up by a dip in his pool. His bedroom had French doors opening onto the patio and pool so he had tracks laid right down to the pool from his room. There he had his bed set on the tracks and a special alarm rigged up. When the alarm went off in the morning, it set his bed to moving down the tracks, and up ended it at the edge of the pool with him waking up when he hit the water.

It's Leap Year
(January, 1948)

Well, folks, I see by the calendar that it's Leap Year again. Another four years have rolled by, and the gals are all busy getting their hunting licenses renewed. It sure is a wonder that the menfolk don't get together and put in a complaint to the Wild Life Commission. Their open season lasts a whole year, and there isn't a duck or a deer in the country that doesn't get a better break than that!

As a matter of fact, I reckon Leap Year's the reason so many Hollywood bachelors have been out shooting everything they could find in the way of a critter that grows its own feathers or furs. They wanted one more last taste of the enjoyment of hunting before the guns got turned on them.

As for shooting more than the legal limit — well, I haven't talked it over with any of the boys but after all, if you're in the pokey for it, you've already had your fun, and it'd take a mighty stalwart female to storm the walls of a modern jail as part of her hunting expedition. The fellas may figure they're better off behind bars.

Maybe someone should warn the gals that they'd better not try any such shenanigans. The legal limit on husbands is still one — at a time, that is — and the rap for bigamy is a lot stiffer than a few dollars fine. Besides, when they're being honest, most women would confess that one husband is plenty to manage. (If there are any husbands around who still think they're not managed, we're only kidding, boys.)

Looks like they'll have to think up some new rules for Leap Year before long. Like the buffalo, yak, deer and other game before him, the human male is growing scarcer and scarcer. The rigors of the chase are harder on the hunter than the hunted, or something. Some expert figured out that at the rate things are going, women will outnumber men two to one before many years have passed. Maybe the Mormons had the right idea, after all.

You can talk all you want to about the beauty of a duck blind in the frosty dawn, or the spectacle of red-coated riders and baying hounds when they're chasing the poor little fox, but I still think there's no sight in the world to compare with the female hunter tracking down her prey.

There she goes: Dressed to the teeth and past them, looking for the world as if that fur coat belonged to her and not to the loan sharks. She's spent five hours in the beauty parlor, and there isn't an inch of her that isn't done to a turn. But somehow she manages to look so casual about it all — "Dahling, what a surprise to see you here! I didn't know you'd be at this party, or I'd have dressed up for the occasion."

Butter wouldn't melt in her mouth, and there's simply nothing in the world she'd rather do than listen to him tell all about himself. That's all, brother! How's he to know that a year from now she'll complain every ten minutes that she hasn't got a thing to wear and he'd better fork over some dough, that she'll be too busy to go to the beauty parlor, and that she won't let him open his yap long enough to say, "Pass the toast, darling"?

Ah, yes, it's a beautiful sight, this manhunt we pretend goes on only one year out of four. Leap Year, kids — the stag's at bay!

Molasses Crumb Pie
(Syndicated June 8, 1947)

I'm not bragging a bit when I say I have the best recipe in Hollywood for an unusual coffee cake. In fact, just ask any of my friends who have sampled my special Molasses Crumb Pie — the way I make it, that is! Three-year-old Juliette and my husband have formed a "Molasses-crumb-pie-once-a-week-or-else" club, and if you've ever had a three-year-old scowling at you, not to mention a scowling husband, you know 'tis better to heed the warning — and go Pennsylvania Dutch for breakfast. I tried for years to vary my breakfast cake — bought every kind on the market, made every possible concoction I could get my hands on — and still they tasted like the usual. Then finally the recipe for Molasses Crumb Pie found its way into my hands (it was sent to me by a Pennsylvania Dutch fan), and now I'd like to pass it on to you.

Here goes for happier breakfasts with Molasses Crumb Pie!

Dissolve three-quarters teaspoon soda in one cup of hot water and stir one-half of the solution into one cup of molasses. Add the remainder of the water and soda to the molasses and continue stirring until foamy.

Mix three cups flour, one cup sugar (white or brown), one teaspoon baking powder with three-quarters cup of butter and lard. Rub this mixture between the fingers to make the crumbs, and keep in a separate bowl. Line three pie plates with pastry and pour in half of the molasses mixture. Add a layer of crumbs. Then pour in the remainder of the mixture and add more of the crumbs. Sprinkle the rest of the crumbs on top of the pies and bake in a hot oven of 375-400 degrees F. This makes three pies — which may seem like two too many, but once you taste them, you'll wish for three more of the same.

Molasses Crumb Pie can double for dessert, too. All "drunkards" will rejoice, for nothing holds the coffee as well as Molasses Crumb Pie.

Credits

Radio

1928, *The Happiness Girls* Songs by Judy and Ann Canova. WJAX-Jacksonville, FL.

January 5, 1936 – December 27, 1936, *Musical Varieties*
Stars Paul Whiteman and his Orchestra. Regular supporting performers included Judy Canova and Morton Downey. Sponsored by Woodbury, Blue Network, Sunday evenings. 9:45 to 10:30 p.m., EST till Aug. 12, 1936 when the series aired 9:15 to 10 p.m., EST

October 11, 1937, *The Grape-Nuts Program*
Stars George Burns and Gracie Allen. Sponsored by Grape-Nuts, NBC, Monday evening from 8 to 8:30 p.m., EST. Judy Canova supposedly replaces a vacationing Bob Burns.

May 26, 1938, *The Royal Gelatin Hour*
Stars Rudy Vallee. Sponsored by Royal Gelatin. Broadcast Thursday evening over NBC. 8 to 9 p.m., EST. Judy Canova and her family perform and yodel.

July 7, 1938, *The Royal Gelatin Hour*
Stars Rudy Vallee. Sponsored by Royal Gelatin. Broadcast Thursday evening over NBC. 8 to 9 p.m., EST. Guest performer Judy Canova performs.

September 15, 1938, *The Royal Gelatin Hour*
Stars Rudy Vallee. Sponsored by Royal Gelatin. Broadcast Thursday evening over NBC. 8 to 9 p.m., EST. Guest performer Judy Canova performs.

October 30, 1938, *The Chase and Sanborn Hour*
Stars Edgar Bergen and Charlie McCarthy. Sponsored by Chase and San-born. NBC. Broadcast Sunday evening from 8 to 9 p.m., EST. Judy Canova is a guest performer for this broadcast, which aired opposite the infamous "War of the Worlds" broadcast.

May 7, 1942, *Command Performance*
Episode #12. This program was recorded but broadcast overseas (not in the U.S.) so the broadcast date varied depending on what part of the world it was broadcast. The date may be the recording date. Canova is among a list of guests, including Robert Benchley and the cast of *The Jack Benny Program*.

(Courtesy of Randy Bonneville. Radio credits courtesy of Martin Grams, Jr.)

June 28, 1942, *The Texaco Star Theatre*
Stars Fred Allen. Sponsored by Texaco Oil and Gas. Broadcast Sunday evening from 9 to 10 p.m. CBS. This was the final episode of the season. Fred and Judy remember vaudeville and perform a duet on a banjo.

October 22, 1942, *The Kraft Music Hall*
Starring Bing Crosby. Sponsored by Kraft Foods. Broadcast Thursday evenings from 9 to 10 p.m. NBC. Judy sings "Some of These Days" with Bing.

November 3, 1942, *Command Performance*
Episode #40. This program was recorded but broadcast overseas (not in the U.S.) so the broadcast date varied depending on what part of the world it was broadcast. The date may be the recording date. Judy opens the show singing "Two Hours After the Crap Game." Also in the guest cast: Edgar Bergen and Kenny Baker.

November 26, 1942, *Elgin Thanksgiving Tribute to Our Armed Forces*
Hour-long special broadcast over the CBS Radio network. Judy Canova appears as a guest with Red Skelton, Gene Krupa, Harriett Hilliard, Loretta Young, and Spike Jones.

January 13, 1943, *It's Time to Smile*
Stars Eddie Cantor. Sponsored by Sal Hepatica. Broadcast Wednesday evening 9 to 9:30 p.m., EST. NBC. Judy is a guest and sings and performs a skit.

March 7, 1943, *The Texaco Star Theatre*
Stars Fred Allen. Sponsored by Texaco Oil and Gas. Broadcast Sunday evening from 9 to 10 p.m. CBS. Judy Canova is a guest.

May 15, 1943, *Command Performance*
Episode #67. This program was recorded but broadcast overseas (not in the U.S.) so the broadcast date varied depending on what part of the world it was broadcast. The date may be the recording date. Judy is among the guests, including Dick Powell, Martha Tilton, Virginia O'Brien, and Eddie "Rochester" Anderson.

July 6, 1943 – June 27, 1944, *Rancho Canova*
Stars Judy Canova. Sponsored by Colgate. Tuesday evenings over CBS. 8:30 – 9 p.m., EST

August 14, 1943, *Command Performance*
Episode #79-A. This program was recorded but broadcast overseas (not in the U.S.) so the broadcast date varied depending on what part of the world it was broadcast. The date may be the recording date. Judy is among the guests which includes Xavier Cugat, Carlos Ramirez, and Jimmy Wakely.

January 6, 1944, *The Abbott and Costello Show*
Sponsored by Camel. Broadcast Thursday evening from 10 to 10:30 p.m., EST. NBC. Lou Costello wants to marry Judy Canova. Mel Blanc also guests.

May 10, 1944, *Mail Call*
Episode #90. This program was recorded but broadcast overseas (not in the U.S.) so the broadcast date varied depending on what part of the world it was broadcast. The date may be the recording date. Judy is among the guests, which included Jerry Colonna.

January 6, 1945 – June 30, 1945, *The Judy Canova Show*
Stars Judy Canova. Sponsored by Colgate. Saturday evenings over NBC. 10 to 10:30 p.m.

February 5, 1945, *The Lady Esther Screen Guild Theatre*
Broadcast over CBS on Monday evenings from 10 to 10:30 p.m., EST. Sponsored by Lady Esther Cosmetics. Judy Canova is a guest with Joe E. Brown for a drama titled "Joan of Ozark," a comedy about a gal from Arkansas who sings against the Nazis and Japanese in New York City.

February 18, 1945, *The Radio Hall of Fame*
Sponsored by Philco. Broadcast over the Blue Network on Sunday evenings. Judy Canova and the cast of *Duffy's Tavern* (except for Ed Gardner) are guests.

March 22, 1945, *Command Performance*
Episode #167. This program was recorded but broadcast overseas (not in the U.S.) so the broadcast date varied depending on what part of the world it was broadcast. The date may be the recording date. Judy is among the guests, which include Dinah Shore and Marilyn Maxwell.

April 29, 1945, *The Harold Lloyd Comedy Theatre*
Sponsored by Old Gold. Broadcast over the Blue Network, broadcast Sunday evenings from 10:30 to 11 p.m., EST. Judy Canova is a guest performer in

an adaptation of *Scatterbrain*, based on the Republic Studios movie of the same name.

July 19, 1945, *Command Performance*
Episode #184. This program was recorded but broadcast overseas (not in the U.S.) so the broadcast date varied depending on what part of the world it was broadcast. The date may be the recording date. Judy is the emcee for this episode.

September 1, 1945 – June 29, 1946, *The Judy Canova Show*
Stars Judy Canova. Sponsored by Colgate. Saturday evenings over NBC. 10 to 10:30 p.m.

November 18, 1945, *Request Performance*
Sponsored by Campbell's Soup. Broadcast Sunday evening from 9 to 9:30 p.m., EST. Guests include Judy Canova and Herbert Marshall. Judy sings "Shortnin' Bread."

December 16, 1945, *The Radio Hall of Fame*
Sponsored by Philco. Broadcast over the ABC Network on Sunday evenings from 6 to 6:30 p.m., EST. Judy Canova, Perry Como, and Martha Tilton are guests.

Circa 1946, *Here's to Veterans*
Episode #100. This program was recorded by the Veterans Administration for troops stationed overseas and broadcast overseas (not in the U.S.) so there is no true broadcast date; it varies depending on what part of the world it was broadcast. The date is the recording date. An excerpt from *The Judy Canova Show* with Judy Canova and Mel Blanc is featured.

August 31, 1946 – June 28, 1947, *The Judy Canova Show*
Stars Judy Canova. Sponsored by Colgate. Saturday evenings over NBC. 10 to 10:30 p.m.

October 14, 1946, *NBC Parade of Stars*
A program in celebration of NBC's 20th Anniversary. A three-hour broadcast from 8 to 11 p.m., EST. Judy Canova is a guest among others, including Bob Hope, Bob Burns, Bill Stern, Perry Como, Art Linkletter, Alice Faye, Alan Young, Ed Gardner, and more.

August 5, 1947, *Command Performance*
Episode #284. This program was recorded but broadcast overseas (not in the U.S.) so the broadcast date varied depending on what part of the world it was broadcast. The date may be the recording date. Judy sings "Why, Oh, Why Did I Ever Leave Wyoming?" Also in the cast: Mel Blanc and David Street.

August 30, 1947 – June 26, 1948, *The Judy Canova Show*
Stars Judy Canova. Sponsored by Colgate. Saturday evenings over NBC. 10 to 10:30 p.m. Broadcast from 9:30 to 10 p.m., EST beginning October 4, 1947.

January 15, 1948, *The 1948 March of Dimes Show*
Three five-minute public service announcements recorded at the NBC Studios, sponsored by the March of Dimes. Syndicated; the date may be the recording date. Guests included Judy Canova, Frank Sinatra, Kay Kyser, and William Bendix. Ralph Edwards was the host.

September 25, 1948, *A Day in the Life of Dennis Day*
Starring Dennis Day. Situation comedy sponsored by Colgate-Palmolive-Peet. Broadcast Saturday evenings over NBC. Judy Canova is a guest who drops by to promote her show which is to be broadcast on the same network.

October 2, 1948 – June 25, 1949, *The Judy Canova Show*
Stars Judy Canova. Sponsored by Colgate. Saturday evenings over NBC. 9:30 to 10 p.m.

January 14, 1949, *The 1949 March of Dimes*
Three five-minute public service announcements recorded at the NBC Studios, sponsored by the March of Dimes. Syndicated; the date may be the recording date. Guests included Judy Canova, Dennis Day, and country singer Spade Cooley.

January 14, 1949, *The 1949 March of Dimes Show*
This fifteen-minute program was recorded at the NBC Studios, and was sponsored by the March of Dimes. Syndicated; the date may be the recording date. Guests included Judy Canova, Frank Sinatra, Kay Kyser and William Bendix. Ralph Edwards was the host.

January 21, 1949, *The Jimmy Durante Show*, a.k.a. *Camel Caravan*
Sponsored by Camel Cigarettes. Stars Jimmy Durante with Alan Young. Broadcast Friday evenings from 8:30 to 9 p.m., EST. Judy Canova was a guest.

January 27, 1949, *The Sealtest Variety Theatre*
Sponsored by Sealtest. Broadcast Thursday evening from 9:30 to 10 p.m.,
EST. NBC. Stars Dorothy Lamour. Guests Alan Reed, Douglas Fairbanks,
Jr., Red Skelton, and Judy Canova make an appeal for the March of Dimes.

October 1, 1949 – July 1, 1950, *The Judy Canova Show*
Stars Judy Canova. Sponsored by Colgate. Saturday evenings over NBC.
9:30 to 10 p.m.

October 7, 1950 – June 30, 1951, *The Judy Canova Show*
Stars Judy Canova. Sponsored by Colgate. Saturday evenings over NBC.
9:30 to 10 p.m.

December 29, 1951 – July 5, 1952, *The Judy Canova Show*
Stars Judy Canova. Sustained. Saturday evenings over NBC. 9 to 9:30 p.m.
EST

April 27, 1952, **One Man's Family Special**
A special 20th Anniversary program for the daytime radio program, *One
Man's Family.* Guests Include Phil Harris, Alice Faye, Bob Hope, Frank
Lovejoy, Joan Banks, and Judy Canova.

September 26, 1952, *The Cascade of Stars*
A special program promoting the new fall line-up on NBC. Thirty-minute
broadcast also featured Judy Canova promoting her own radio program.

October 8, 1952, **Tandem Productions Advertising Campaign**
A not-for-broadcast closed circuit transmission or syndicated sales presen-
tation for NBC's fall sales campaign. The fifteen-minute program featured
Judy Canova, William Gargan, and Red Skelton.

October 23, 1952 – May 28, 1953, *The Judy Canova Show*
Stars Judy Canova. Multiple sponsors. Thursday evenings over NBC. 10 to
10:30 p.m. EST

January 2, 1957, **Recollections at Thirty**
A nostalgic look at the era of radio broadcasts, featuring excepts from a
variety of programs. NBC. Broadcast from Wednesday from 8:30 to 9 p.m.,
EST. Excerpt from one of Judy's appearances on the Rudy Vallee program
is highlighted.

Undated Recordings
Judy Canova Monologues and Recipes was a series of ten-minute recordings produced by World Transcription/World Program Service Transcription. At least 158 recordings were made.

Feature Films

In Caliente (1935) D: Lloyd Bacon.
Dolores Del Rio, Pat O'Brien, Leo Carrillo, Edward Everett Horton, Glenda Farrell, Phil Regan, Winifred Shaw, Luis Alberni, George Humbert, Harry Holman, Soledad Jimenez, Herman Bing, The Canovas [Judy, Annie, Pete, Zeke], The DeMarcos, Katherine de Mille, Dorothy Dare.
Released on May 25.
Warner Bros./First National (84 min.)

It's not easy at first, but a romance manages to develop between magazine critic O'Brien and hot-tempered Latin dancer Del Rio — to whom he gave an unfavorable review. Judy makes her feature film debut doing a novelty reprise of "The Lady in Red" following Shaw's rendition. Choreography by Busby Berkeley. From the story "Caliente" by Warren Duff and Ralph Block. Filmed in Tijuana, Baja California Norte, Mexico.

Songs:
"In Caliente" *(Allie Wrubel-Mort Dixon)*
"The Lady in Red" *(Wrubel-Dixon)*
"To Call You My Own" *(Wrubel-Dixon)*
"Muchacha" *(Harry Warren-Al Dubin)*
"Mexicana" *(Wrubel-Dixon)*
"When Irish Eyes Are Smiling" *(Ernest Ball-Chauncey Olcott-George Graff)*
"She's A Latin from Manhattan" *(Warren-Dubin)*
"Tango Muchacha" *(Warren)*
Music by Leo F. Forbstein, Bernhard Kaun

Broadway Gondolier (1935) D: Lloyd Bacon.
Dick Powell, Joan Blondell, Adolphe Menjou, Louise Fazenda, William Gargan, George Barbier, Grant Mitchell, Ted Fio Rito and His Band, The Four Mills Brothers [Donald, Harry, Herbert, John], Hobart Cavanaugh, Joseph Sauers [Sawyer], Rafael Storm, Bob Murphy, James Burke, The

Canova Family [Judy, Annie, Pete, Zeke], Jack Norton, Candy Candido, George Chandler, Henry Da Silva, Bill [William] Elliott, June Travis.
Released on July 27.
Warner Bros. (98 min.)

Cab driver Powell yearns to be a successful radio singer, so his two lady friends (Blondell, Fazenda) concoct a scheme to get him discovered — but he has to travel to Venice first. Judy Canova does a hillbilly specialty number with her family.

Songs:
"Flagenheim's Odorless Cheese" *(Harry Warren-Al Dubin)*
"Outside Of You" *(Warren-Dubin)*
"The Pig and the Cow *(And The Dog and the Cat)*" *(Warren-Dubin)*
"Lonely Gondolier" *(Warren-Dubin, with Italian lyrics by Manuel Emanuel)*
"The Rose in Her Hair" *(Warren-Dubin, with Italian lyrics by Emanuel)*
"Lulu's Back in Town" *(Warren-Dubin)*
"You Can Be Kissed" *(Warren-Dubin)*
"Sweet And Low" *(Warren-Dubin)*
"About A Quarter To Nine" *(Warren-Dubin)*
Music by Ray Heindorf, Heinz Roemheld

Going Highbrow (1935) D: Robert Florey.
Guy Kibbee, ZaSu Pitts, Edward Everett Horton, Ross Alexander, June Martel, Gordon Westcott, Judy Canova, Nella Walker, Jack Norton, Arthur Treacher, Irving Back [Bacon], Gordon [William] Elliott.
Released on August 23.
Warner Bros. (67 min.)

To make the right impression while trying to break into high society, a husband and wife (Kibbee and Pitts) are advised to throw a coming-out party for their non-existent daughter. They hire a waitress to pose as their offspring. Judy plays Annie. From the play *Social Pirates* by Ralph Spence.

Songs:
"One In A Million" *(Louis Alter-Jack Scholl)*
"Moon Crazy" *(Alter-Scholl)*
Music by Bernhard Kaun, Heinz Roemheld

Artists & Models (1937) D: Raoul Walsh.
Jack Benny, Ida Lupino, Richard Arlen, Gail Patrick, Ben Blue, Judy Canova, The Yacht Club Boys [George Kelly, Charles Adler, William B. Mann, James V. Kern], Cecil Cunningham, Donald Meek, Hedda Hopper, Ann & Zeke Canova, Martha Raye, The Andre Kostelanetz Orchestra, Russell Patterson's Personettos, The Louis Armstrong Orchestra, Connee Boswell, Rube Goldberg, Madelon Grey, Alan Birmingham, Kathryn Kay, Del Henderson, David Newell.
Released on August 13 (one of the 38 top-grossing films of 1936-37).
Paramount (97 min./Western Electric Mirrophonic Recording)

Several acts are on hand in this story about Lupino's pose as a socialite and ad-man Benny's search for the right girl to represent his silverware company. Judy Canova plays Toots and joins her siblings (Ann, Zeke) for a specialty number.

Songs:
"Sasha Pasha Sasha" *(The Yacht Club Boys – Ted Koehler)*
"Pop Goes The Bubble (And Soap Gets In My Eyes)" *(Burton Lane-Koehler)* sung by Judy Canova
"Whispers In The Dark" *(Frederick Hollander-Leo Robin)* Academy Award Nominee – Best Song
"Stop! You're Breaking My Heart" *(Lane-Koehler)* sung by Judy Canova, Ben Blue
"Public Melody No. 1" *(Harold Arlen-Koehler)*
"Mr. Esquire" *(Victor Young-Koehler)* instrumental
"I Have Eyes" *(Ralph Rainger-Robin)*
"Moonlight and Shadows" *(Hollander-Robin)*
Music by Victor Young (and Robert Russell Bennett, Gordon Jenkins, John Leipold, Leo Shuken)

Thrill Of A Lifetime (1937) D: George Archainbaud.
The Yacht Club Boys [George Kelly, William B. Mann, James V. Kern], Judy Canova, Ben Blue, Eleanore Whitney, Johnny Downs, Betty Grable, Leif Erickson, Larry [Buster] Crabbe, Zeke & Ann Canova, Tommy Wonder, Franklin Pangborn, Si Jenks, Howard M. Mitchell, Billy Daniels, Joyce Mathews, Marjorie Reynolds.
Released on December 3.
Paramount (72 min.)

As a summer stock company organizes a show they hope will land on Broadway, a secretary falls for her handsome playwright boss. Judy Canova is seen as Judy. Choreography by LeRoy Prinz.

Songs:
"Merry Go Round" *(The Yacht Club Boys)*
"It's Been a Whole Year" *(The Yacht Club Boys)*
"Sweetheart Time" *(Frederick Hollander-Sam Coslow)*
"Thrill of a Lifetime" *(Hollander-Coslow)*
"Nobody's Darling" *(Jimmie Davis)*
"Paris in Swing" *(Hollander-Coslow)*
"If We Could Run the Country for a Day" *(The Yacht Club Boys)*
"Blow the Whistle" *(Harry McClintock-Sterling Sherwin)*
"Keeno, Screeno and You" *(Hollander-Coslow)*
"I'll Follow My Baby" *(Hollander-Coslow)*
Music by Gordon Jenkins, John Leipold, Arthur Franklin, Boris Morros, Carlos Romeros, Victor Young.

Scatterbrain (1940) D: Gus Meins.
Judy Canova, Alan Mowbray, Ruth Donnelly, Eddie Foy Jr., Joseph Cawthorn, Wallace Ford, Isabel Jewell, Luis Alberni, Billy Gilbert, Emmett Lynn, Jimmy Starr, The Matty Malneck Orchestra, The KCBS Texas Rangers [Robert 'Captain Bob' Crawford, Edward 'Tookie' Cronenbold, Francis 'Irish' Mahaney, Roderic 'Dave' May], Cal Shrum's Gang, Marion Martin, Cliff Nazarro, Herb Vigran, Johnny Arthur, Billy Bletcher, Dick Elliott.
Released on July 20.
Republic (74 min./RCA Sound)

Ozark gal Canova (as Judy Hull) finds herself going to Hollywood when she is discovered by film producer Cawthorn.

Songs:
"Benny the Beaver" *(Hy Heath-Johnny Lange-Lew Porter)*
"Scatterbrain" *(Keene Bean-Frankie Masters-Johnny Burke)*
"Scatterbrain Finale" *(Jule Styne-George Brown-Sol Meyer)*
"She'll Be Comin' 'Round the Mountain" *(Traditional)*
"Ciribiribin" *(Alberto Pestalozza-Harry James-Jack Lawrence)*
"I Ain't Got Nobody" *(Roger Graham-Spencer Williams)*
Music by Cy Feuer.

Sis Hopkins (1941) D: Joseph Santley.
Judy Canova, Bob Crosby, Charles Butterworth, Jerry Colonna, Susan Hayward, Katharine Alexander, Elvia Allman, Carol Adams, Lynn Merrick, Mary Ainslee, Charles Coleman, Andrew Tombes, Charles Lane, Byron Foulger, Betty Blythe, Frank Darien, Joe Devlin, Elliott Sullivan, Hal Price, Anne O'Neal, The Bobcats.
Released on April 12.
Republic (98 min./RCA Sound)

Canova (in the title role) is taken in by her well-to-do uncle's family when her country farm burns down. She attends the same college as her snooty cousin (Hayward) and becomes popular despite Susan's social sabotage. From the play by Carroll Fleming and George A. Nichols.

Songs:
"That Ain't Hay" *(Jule Styne-Frank Loesser)* sung by Canova
"Alma Mater" *(Styne)*
"Well! Well!" *(Styne-Loesser)*
"Look At You, Look At Me" *(Styne-George Brown-Loesser)*
"Here We Are Studying History" *(Styne-Loesser)*
"Cleopatra" *(Styne-Loesser)*
"If You're In Love" *(Styne-Loesser)*
"Some of These Days" *(Shelton Brooks)*
"Ah Fors A Lui" from *La Traviata (Giuseppe Verdi)* sung by Canova
"Sugar Foot Stomp" *(Joe Oliver-Louis Armstrong)*
"South Rampart Street Parade" *(Steve Allen-Ray Bauduc-Bob Haggart)*
"Wait for the Wagon" *(George P. Khauf-R. Bishop Buckley)*
Music by Cy Feuer, *(Mort Glickman, Walter Scharf)*

Puddin' Head (1941) D: Joseph Santley.
Judy Canova, Francis Lederer, Raymond Walburn, Slim Summerville, Astrid Allwyn, Eddie Foy Jr., Alma Kruger, Hugh O'Connell, Chick Chandler, Paul Harvey, Nora Lane, Gerald Oliver Smith, Wendell Niles, Vince Barnett, Betty Blythe, The Sportsmen [Bill Days, John Rarig, Thurl Ravenscroft, Max Smith].
Released on June 25.
Republic (80 min.)

City farmer Canova (as Judy Goober) deals with a pair of slick con-men and wins herself a radio singing contract.

Songs:

"Minnie Hotcha" *(Jule Styne-Eddie Cherkose)* sung by Canova
"Puddin' Head" *(Sol Meyer-Styne-Cherkose)*
"Hey Junior" *(Styne-Cherkose)* sung by Canova
"You're Tellin' I" *(Styne-Cherkose)* sung by Canova
"Manhattan Holiday" *(Styne-Cherkose)* sung by Canova
"Ghost Routine" *(Styne-Cherkose)*
Music by Cy Feuer, (Walter Scharf, Mort Glickman)

Sleepytime Gal (1942) D: Albert S. Rogell.
Judy Canova, Tom Brown, Billy Gilbert, Ruth Terry, Thurston Hall, Elisha
Cook Jr., Jerry Lester, Mildred Coles, Harold Huber, Fritz Feld, Frank Sully,
Jimmy Ames, Jay Novello, The Skinnay Ennis Orchestra, Paul Fix, Vicki
Lester, Mady Lawrence, Lester Dorr, Walter Merrill, Pat Gleason, Fred
Santley, Edward Earle, Hillary Brooke, Cyril Ring, Rick Vallin, Gertrude
Astor, Eddie Acuff, Carl Leviness, William Forrest, Marguerite Whitten,
Dwight Frye, Eugene Borden.
Released on March 5.
Republic (84 min./RCA Sound)

Canova (as Bessie Cobb) finds herself in danger when she is targeted by mob-
sters; they've mistaken her for a nightclub singer they want to rub out.

Songs:
"I Don't Want Anybody At All" *(Jule Styne-Herb Magidson)* sung by
    Canova
"When The Cat's Away" *(Styne-Magidson)* sung by Canova
"Barrelhouse Bessie" *(Styne-Magidson)* sung by Canova
"Sleepytime Gal" *(Ange Lorenzo-Richard A. Whiting-J.R. Alden-Richard B.*
    Egan) sung by Canova
Music by Cy Feuer, Gene Rose

True To The Army (1942) D: Albert [S.] Rogell.
Judy Canova, Allan Jones, Ann Miller, Jerry Colonna, Clarence Kolb, Edward
Pawley, William Wright, William Demarest, Edwin Miller, Arthur Loft,
Gordon Jones, Rod Cameron, Eddie Acuff, Edgar Dearing, Mary Treen,
Selmer Jackson, John Miljan, Harry Barris, Frank Sully, Joseph Crehan,
George Turner, Dorothy Sebastian, Donald Kerr, Ralph Dunn, Stanley
Blystone, Syd Saylor.

Released on March 21.
Paramount (76 min./video/DVD)

Entertainer Canova (as Daisy Hawkins) flees from gangsters and puts military discipline to the test when she takes refuge at an all-male camp. Complications abound as she attempts to hide her gender from officers. Taken from *She Loves Me Not*, both a novel (by Edward Hope Coffey Jr.) and play (by Howard Lindsay).

Songs:
"In The Army" *(Harold Spina-Frank Loesser)*
"Spangles On My Tights" *(Spina-Loesser)*
"Need I Speak?" *(Spina-Loesser)*
"Swing In Line" *(Joseph J. Lilley-Loesser)*
"Jitterbug's Lullaby" *(Spina-Loesser)*
"Wacki From Khaki" *(Spina-Loesser)*
"Love In Bloom" *(Ralph Rainger-Leo Robin)* sung by Canova
Music by Joseph J. Lilley, Jimmy McHugh, Victor Young

Joan Of Ozark (1942) D: Joseph Santley.
Judy Canova, Joe E. Brown, Eddie Foy Jr., Jerome Cowan, Alexander Granach, Anne Jeffreys, Otto Reichow, Donald Curtis, Wolfgang Zilzer, Hans von Twardowski, Harry Hayden, William Vaughn, William Dean, Paul Fung, Olin Howlin, George Eldredge, Ralph Peters, Emmett Lynn, Chester Clute, Kam Tong, Cyril Ring, Eric Alden, Ralph McCullough, Lloyd Whitlock, Bud Jamison, Bob Stevenson, Peppy & Peanuts Walters, Jason Robards [Sr.], Charles Williams.
Released on July 15.
Republic (80 min.)

Quail-hunting Canova (as Judy Hull) inadvertently gets mixed up with Nazi spies when she brings down a pigeon carrying messages to operatives in America.

Songs:
"Pull The Trigger" *(Harry Revel-Mort Greene)*
"Backwoods Barbeque" *(Revel-Greene)*
"Lady At Lockheed" *(Revel-Greene)*
"Dixie" *(Revel-Greene)*
"Wabash Blues" *(Dave Ringle-Fred Meinken)*
Music by Cy Feuer, Gene Rose, (Mort Glickman)

Chatterbox (1943) D: Joseph Santley.
Joe E. Brown, Judy Canova, Rosemary Lane, John Hubbard, Gus Shilling, Chester Clute, Anne Jeffreys, Emmett Vogan, George Byron, Billy Bletcher, The Mills Brothers [Herbert, Harry, Donald, John Sr.], The Spade Cooley Orchestra, Roy Barcroft, Marie Windsor, Pierce Lyden, Robert 'Buzz' Henry, Earle Hodgins.
Released on April 27.
Republic (76 min./RCA Sound/DVD)

Brown stars as a radio cowboy who cannot ride a horse in real life. This causes a real dilemma when he's signed to do a film. Canova plays Judy Boggs, the gal who tries to help him out. Filmed at Iverson Ranch, Chatsworth, CA.

Songs:
"Welcome To Victory Ranch" *(Harry Akst-Sol Meyer)*
"Mad About Him, Sad Without Him, How Can I Be Glad Without Him Blues" *(Larry Markes-Dick Charles)*
"Sweet Lucy Brown" *(Lou Rene-Otis Rene)*
"Why Can't I Sing A Love Song" *(Akst-Meyer)*
Music by Walter Scharf

Sleepy Lagoon (1943) D: Joseph Santley.
Judy Canova, Dennis Day, Ruth Donnelly, Joe Sawyer, Ernest Truex, Douglas Fowley, Will Wright, Herbert Corthell, Ellen Lowe, Forrest Taylor, Kitty McHugh, Eddy Chandler, Jack Raymond, Margaret Reid, The Mike Riley Orchestra, Sammy Stein, Jack Kenney, Eddie Gribbon, Jay Novello, Emil Van Horn, Rondo Hatton, James Farley. Narrated by Frank Graham.
Released on September 5.
Republic (65 min./RCA Sound)

Seeking to bring law and order to the title town, determined Canova (as Judy Joyner) runs for public office so she can go after crooked mayor Wright. From the novel *The Miracle of Sleepy Hollow* by Prescott Chaplin.

Songs:
"If You Are There" *(Phil Ohman-Ned Washington)*
"You're The Fondest Thing I Am Of" *(Ohman-Washington)* sung by Canova, Sawyer
"I'm Not Myself Anymore" *(Ohman-Washington)*

"Political Satire" *(Ohman-Washington)*
"Sleepy Lagoon" *(E. Coates-Jack Lawrence)*
Music by Walter Scharf, (Johnny Green, Inez James)

Louisiana Hayride (1944) D: Charles Barton.
Judy Canova, Ross Hunter, Richard Lane, Lloyd Bridges, Matt Willis, George McKay, Minerva Urecal, Hobart Cavanaugh, Russell Hicks, Eddie Kane, Walter Baldwin, Nelson Leigh, Arthur Loft, Si Jenks, Syd Saylor, Bud Jamison, Ernie Adams, Jack Rice, Lane Chandler, Eddy Chandler, Frank Hagney, Christine McIntyre, Jessie Arnold, Gene Roth, Art Miles.
Released on July 13.
Columbia (67 min.)

A chick from the sticks (Canova, as Judy Crocker) has to deal with a pair of conmen out to steal oil-rich property before she can pursue her dream of making it big in Hollywood. Mel Ferrer was dialogue coach.

Songs:
"You Gotta Go Where the Train Goes" *(Walter Kent-Kim Gannon)* sung by
    Canova
"Rainbow Road" *(Kent-Gannon)* sung by Canova
"I'm a Woman of the World" *(Saul Chaplin-Jerry Seelen)*
"Put Your Arms Around Me Honey" *(Albert Von Tilzer-Junie McCree)*
"Shortnin' Bread" *(Jacques Wolfe-Clement Wood)* sung by Canova
Music by Saul Chaplin, M.R. [Mischa] Bakaleinikoff, (Leigh Harline, Ben
    Oakland, George Parrish, Paul Sawtell)

Hit The Hay (1945) D: Del Lord.
Judy Canova, Ross Hunter, Fortunio Bonanova, Doris Merrick, Gloria Holden, Francis Pierlot, Grady Sutton, Louis Mason, Paul Stanton, Clyde Fillmore, Maurice Cass, Luis Alberni, Cosmo Sardo, William Newell.
Released on November 25.
(75 min.) Columbia

Hillbilly Canova (as Judy Stevens) enters the world of opera with a fine voice but no acting ability; she pairs with a look-alike actress (also played by Canova) who can act, but not sing. Canova's stunt double was Mary Adams Hayes.

Songs:
"Martha" *(excerpts) (Flowtow)*
"Tille Tell" *(re-orchestration of Gioacchino Rossini's "William Tell")*
Arias from "Rigoletto" *(Giuseppi Verdi)*, "La Traviata" *(Verdi)*, "The Barber
   Of Seville" *(Rossini) (all sung by Canova)*
"No Other Love"
"Old McDonald Had A Farm" *(Traditional)*
Music by Marlin Skiles.

Singin' In The Corn (1946) D: Del Lord.
Judy Canova, Allen Jenkins, Guinn 'Big Boy' Williams, Alan Bridge, Charles
Halton, Robert Dudley, Nick Thompson, Frances Rey, George Chesebro,
Ethan Laidlaw, Frank Lackteen, Guy Beach, Jay Silverheels, Rodd Redwing,
Dick Stanley, Charles Randolph, Si Jenks, Pat O'Malley, Chester Conklin,
Mary Gordon, The Singing Indian Braves.
Released on December 26.
Columbia (64 min.)

Carnival mind-reader Canova (as Judy McCoy) works to return a western
ghost town to the Indians so she can inherit a relative's estate.

Songs:
"I'm A Gal Of Property" *(Doris Fisher-Allan Roberts)* sung by Canova
"Pepita Chiquita" *(Fisher-Roberts)*
"Ma, He's Makin' Eyes at Me" *(Con Conrad-Sydney Clare)*
Music by George Duning, *(Hans Sommer)*

Honeychile (1951) D: R.G. Springsteen.
Judy Canova, Eddie Foy Jr., Alan Hale Jr., Walter Catlett, Claire Carleton,
Karolyn Grimes, Brad Morrow, Roy Barcroft, Leonid Kinsky, Gus Shilling,
Irving Bacon, Fuzzy Knight, Roscoe Ates, Ida Moore, Sarah Edwards, Emory
Parnell, Dick Elliott, Dick Wessel, William Fawcett, Robin Winans, Stanley
Blystone, Donia Bussey, John Crawford, Cecil Elliott, Cecil Weston.
Released on October 20.
Republic (90 min./Trucolor)

Canova (as Judy) is a rural songwriter whose composition catches the interest of music publishers; she and boyfriend Hale are also involved with a fixed
chuck-wagon race.

Songs:
"Honeychile" *(Harold Spina-Jack Elliott)* sung by Canova
"Rag Mop" *(Johnnie Wills-Deacon Anderson)* sung by Canova
"More Than I Care To Remember" *(Matt Terry-Ted Johnson)* sung by
     Canova
"Tutti Fruitti" *(Ann Canova-Elliott)* *(sung by Judy Canova)*
Music by Victor Young.

Oklahoma Annie (1952) D: R.G. Springsteen.
Judy Canova, John Russell, Grant Withers, Roy Barcroft, Emmett Lynn,
Frank Ferguson, Minerva Urecal, Houseley Stevenson, Almira Sessions,
Allen Jenkins, Maxine Gates, Emory Parnell, Denver Pyle, House Peters Jr.,
Andrew Tombes, Fuzzy Knight, Si Jenks, Marian Martin, Herbert Vigran,
Hal Price, Fred Hoose, Lee Phelps, Bobby Taylor, William Fawcett.
Released on March 24.
Republic (90min./RCA Sound/Trucolor/video)

Storekeeper Canova (as herself) is sweet on the handsome new sheriff (Russell), and becomes his deputy when she captures a bank robber. Together, they work to foil the town's crooked elements.

Songs:
"Have You Ever Been Lonely" *(George Brown-Peter DeRose)*
"Blow the Whistle" *(Harry McClintock-Sterling Sherwin)*
"Never, Never, Never" *(Sonny Burke-Jack Elliott)*
Music by Nathan Scott.

The Wac From Walla Walla (1952) D: William Witney.
Judy Canova, Stephen Dunne, George Cleveland, June Vincent, Irene Ryan,
Roy Barcroft, Allen Jenkins, George Chandler, Elizabeth Slifer, Thurston
Hall, Sarah Spencer, Dick Wessel, Pattee Chapman, The Republic Rhythm
Riders, Dick Elliott, Carl 'Alfalfa' Switzer, Tom Powers, Jarma Lewis, Emlen
Davies, Virginia Carroll, Evelynne Smith, Phyllis Kennedy, Tweeny [Julieta]
Canova, Juliana Hughes (as pre-teen Judy).
Released on October 10.
Republic (83 min.)

Judy Canova (as herself) accidentally joins the military, but makes herself useful by catching spies out to steal the plans for a new guided missile.

Songs:
"Song Of The Women's Army Corps" *(Harold Spina-Jack Elliott)*
"Boy, Oh Boy" *(Elliott)*
"Lovey" *(Elliott)*
"If Only Dreams Came True" *(Elliott)*
Music by R. Dale Butts.

Untamed Heiress (1954) D: Charles Lamont.
Judy Canova, Donald Barry, George Cleveland, Taylor Holmes, Chick Chandler, Jack Kruschen, Hugh Sanders, Douglas Fowley, William Haade, Ellen Corby, Dick Wessel, James Flavin, Tweeny [Juliette] Canova.
Released on April 12.
Republic (70 min./RCA Sound)

A former prospector, now wealthy, returns to find the woman he once loved. However, she has since died — but he locates her daughter (Judy Canova, as Judy), only to discover she is mixed up with gangsters.

Songs (all sung by Judy Canova):
"Welcome" *(Jack Elliott)*
"A Dream For Sale" *(Elliott-Donald Kahn)*
"Sugar Daddy" *(Kahn-Elliott)*
Music by Stanley Wilson.

Carolina Cannonball (1955) D: Charles Lamont.
Judy Canova, Andy Clyde, Ross Elliott, Sig Rumann, Leon Askin, Jack Kruschen, Frank Wilcox, Emil Sitka, Roy Barcroft.
Released on January 28.
Republic (74 min./RCA Sound/video)

Canova (playing herself) operates a ghost-town trolley with her grandfather (Clyde). Their lives are disrupted when a guided missile inadvertently lands in their backyard and three enemy agents show up to find it.

Songs:
"Carolina Cannonball" *(Donald Kahn-Jack Elliott)* sung by Canova
"Wishin' And Waitin'" *(Kahn-Elliott)* sung by Canova
"Busy As A Beaver" *(Kahn-Elliott)*

Lay That Rifle Down (1955) D: Charles Lamont.
Judy Canova, Robert Lowery, Jil Jarmyn, Jacqueline de Wit, Richard Deacon, Robert Burton, James Bell, Leon Tyler, Tweeny [Juliette] Canova, Pierre Watkin, Marjorie Bennett, William Fawcett, Paul E. Burns, Edmund Cobb, Donald MacDonald, Mimi Gibson, Rudy Lee.
Released on July 7.
Republic (71 min./RCA Sound/DVD)

Judy Canova (as herself) labors in a hotel under the lash of her mean old aunt. Dreaming of a better life, Judy unknowingly gets the attention of swindlers who target the old crone's wealth. Filmed at Iverson Ranch, Chatsworth, California.

Songs:
"The Continental Correspondence Charm School" *(Jack Elliott–Donald Kahn)*
"Sleepy Serenade" *(Elliott–Kahn)*
"I'm Glad I Was Born on My Birthday" *(Elliott–Kahn)*
Music by R. Dale Butts.

The Adventures of Huckleberry Finn (1960) D: Michael Curtiz.
Tony Randall, Eddie Hodges, Patty McCormack, Archie Moore, Neville Brand, Mickey Shaughnessy, Judy Canova, Andy Devine, Sherry Jackson, Buster Keaton, Finlay Currie, Josephine Hutchinson, Parley Baer, John Carradine, Royal Dano, Dolores Hawkins, Sterling Holloway, [Harry] Dean Stanton, Henry Corden, Sam McDaniel, Burt Mustin, Minerva Urecal.
Released on August 3.
Formosa/Metro-Goldwyn-Mayer (107 min./Westrex Recording/Metrocolor/ CinemaScope/video/DVD)

A rambunctious country boy (Hodges) skips school and chores to raft down the Mississippi River with a runaway slave. Canova appears as the sheriff's wife. From the novel by Mark Twain. Produced by Samuel Goldwyn, Jr. Filmed in the Sacramento River Valley, CA and at Stockton Deepwater Channel, Stockton, CA.

Songs:
"Huckleberry Finn" *(Burton Lane–Alan Jay Lerner)*
"I Ain't Never Felt So Good Before" *(Lane–Lerner)*
"I'll Wait For You By The River" *(Lane–Lerner)*
"Pittsburgh Blue" *(Lane–Lerner)*

Golden Laurel Award Nomination, Top Male Supporting Performance –
Tony Randall (5th place).
Music by Jerome Moross.

Cannonball (1976) D: Paul Bartel.
David Carradine, Bill McKinney, Veronica Hamel, Gerrit Graham, Robert
Carradine, Belinda Belaski, Judy Canova, Archie Hahn, Carl Gottlieb,
Mary Woronov, Diane Lee Hart, Glynn Rubin, James Keach, Dick Miller,
Stanley Clay, Louisa Moritz, Allan Arkush, Paul Bartel, Roger Corman,
Joe Dante, Jonathan Kaplan, Aron Kincaid, Martin Scorsese, Sylvester
Stallone.
Released on July 6.
Cross Country/Harbor/Shaw Brothers/New World (93 min./Metrocolor/Rated
PG/video/DVD)

A cross-country road race without rules has prize-hungry drivers burning
rubber and crashing their way to the finish. Canova is seen as Sharma Capri.
Produced by Roger Corman. Filmed on the Harbor Freeway, Los Angeles,
California.

Song:
"He's Just a Man" *(David A. Axelrod-Delaney Bramlett)*
Music by David A. Axelrod.

Short Subjects

The Song Of Fame (1934) D: Joseph Henabery.
Ruth Etting, Eddie Bruce, Arthur Donaldson, Jackson Halliday, Pat West,
The Canovas [Annie, Judy, Andy, Zeke], Minor & Root, Gerald Kent, Charles
La Torre.
Released on July 7.
Vitaphone/Warner Bros. (19 min.)

Etting is featured as a singing cigarette girl who loses her job and hopes to
hit it big by catching the ear of an impresario. Judy Canova performs with
her siblings.

Songs:
"Shine On, Harvest Moon" *(Nora Bayes-Jack Norworth)*
"Tambourine Waltz" *(Hess)*
"I Cried For You" *(Arthur Freed-Gus Arnheim-Abe Lyman)*
"Let's Dance" *(Hess)*
"Mountaineer's Courtship"
"Who Back Buck"
"If I Didn't Care" *(Young-Ager)*
"I Wanna Be Loved" *(Heyman-Green)*
"Finesse" *(Maltin-Doll)*

Meet Roy Rogers (1941) D: Harriet Parsons.
Roy Rogers, Trigger (a horse), George 'Gabby' Hayes, Gene Autry, Judy Canova, Bill [William] Elliott, Bob Baker, Billy Gilbert, Roscoe Ates, Mary Lee. Narrated by Harriet Parsons.
Released on June 24.
Republic (10 min./RCA Sound)

Canova appears as herself in this featurette spotlighting cowboy star Rogers. Entry in the *Meet The Stars* series (#7).

Stars Past And Present (1941) D: Harriet Parsons.
Walter Abel, Gene Autry, Binnie Barnes, Richard Bennett, Jack Buetel, Smiley Burnette, Mae Busch, Judy Canova, Chester Conklin, Minta Durfee, Sally Eilers, William Farnum, Eddie Gribbon, George "Gabby" Hayes, Brenda Joyce, Edgar Kennedy, The Keystone Cops, Mary Lee, Mary Martin, Ilona Massey, Walter McGrail, Ann Miller, Patricia Morison, Jack Mulhall, Charlie Murray, Sr., William T. Orr, Eddie Quillan, Charles Ray, Cesar Romero, Wesley Ruggles, Jane Russell, Mack Sennett, Eddie Sutherland, John Wayne. Narrated by Harriet Parsons.
Released on July 24.
Republic (9 min.)

Canova is one of the movie neophytes who shares the celluloid with veteran players in this *Meet The Stars* opus. It's all about the new sound-stage dedication at Republic Studios (formerly the Mack Sennett Studios), which was dedicated to the memory of the late screen star, Mabel Normand.

Radio Shows (1945) D: Ralph Staub.
Brian Aherne, Barbara Jo Allen, Louise Arthur, Mel Blanc, Judy Canova, Eddie Cantor, Cass Daley, Kay Kyser, Wendell Niles, Ginny Simms, Harry Von Zell, Harlow Wilcox.
Released on October 11.
Columbia (10 min.)

A behind-the-scenes look at a few radio programs and their stars. Canova and Blanc are seen from *The Judy Canova Show*. Entry in the *Screen Snapshots* series (Season 25, No. 2).

Fashions And Rodeo (1945) D: Ralph Staub.
Dusty Anderson, Judy Canova, Leo Carrillo, Jinx Falkenburg, The Robert Mitchell Boys Choir, Michael O'Shea, Shirley Ross, Jane Withers.
Released on November 15.
Columbia (9 min.)

This *Screen Snapshots* series entry (Season 25, No. 3) spotlights a Hollywood fashion show, the singing Mitchell Boys Choir and highlights of actor Carrillo's annual rodeo. Canova is seen as herself.

Radio Characters Of 1946/The Judy Canova Radio Show (1946)
D: Ralph Staub.
Judy Canova, Mel Blanc, Ruby Dandridge, Verna Felton, Howard Petrie.
Released on May 23.
Columbia (11 min.)

The *Screen Snapshots* camera drops in at NBC to view Canova's popular Saturday night radio comedy show. Entry No. 9 of Season 25.

Famous Hollywood Mothers (1947) D: Ralph Staub.
Judy Canova, Brenda Marshall, Eleanor Powell, Rosalind Russell, Ginny Simms.
Released on May 1.
Columbia (10 min.)

Five celebrity moms (including Canova) and their children are visited by the *Screen Snapshots* crew.

Stage

Calling All Stars (1934-35) D: Lew Brown.
Phil Baker, Ella Logan, Everett Marshall, Mitzi Mayfair, Harry McNaughton, Gertrude Niesen, Martha Raye, The Canovas [Ann, Judy, Pete, Zeke], Lou Holtz, The Sara Mildred Strauss Dancers, Arthur Auerbach, Pat C. Flick, D. Raymond.
Opened on December 13.
Hollywood Theater [Times Square Church] (36 performances)

A revue with music, dance and sketches. Judy plays Abbey. Sketches include "Last of the Hillbillies" (performed by Auerbach, The Canovas, Flick, Raymond); "Streamline"; "Absent-Minded Doctor"; "So This is Hollywood"; "The Hiker"; "Lethargy" and "The Stein-Way."
Harry Akst-Lew Brown

Songs:
"Opening"
"Calling All Stars"
"When Are Ya Comin' To See Me?" performed by Judy Canova, Holtz
"I've Nothing to Offer" *(with dance)*
"Just Mention Joe" *(with dance)*
"If It's Love" performed by Judy Canova, Logan, Raye, Whiting
"Straw Hat in The Rain"
"My Old Hoss"
"Thinking Out Loud"
"I Don't Want to Be President"
"I'd Like to Dunk You in My Coffee"
"I'm Stepping Out of the Picture"
"He Just Beats a Tom-Tom"
Music by Al Goodman, Hans Spialek, Conrad Salinger.

Ziegfeld Follies of 1936 (1936) D: Frederick De Cordova.
Fanny Brice, Bob Hope, Gertrude Niesen, Eve Arden, Gene Ashley, Josephine Baker, Milton Barnett, Judy Canova, Harriet Hoctor, The Nicholas Brothers, Hugh O'Connell, June Preisser.
Opened on January 30.
Winter Garden Theater (115 performances)

Another revue for Judy (who plays in three sketches): "The Gazooka" (as Mother), "Amateur Night" (as Elvira McIntosh) and "The Petrified Elevator" (as Anxious Girl). Other sketches: "The Sweepstakes Ticket"; "Fancy! Fancy!"; "Baby Snooks Goes Hollywood"; "Of Thee I Spend"; "Words Without Music"; "5 a.m."; "Moment of Moments" and "Time Marches On." Ballets by George Balanchine. Choreography by Robert Alton.
Vernon Duke-Ira Gershwin

Songs:
"Time Marches On"
"He Hasn't a Thing Except Me"
"(My) Red Letter Day"
"(Island in the) West Indies"
"Words Without Music"
"The Economic Situation (Aren't You Wonderful)"
"Fancy! Fancy!"
"Night Flight"
"Maharanee (At the Night Races in Paris)"
"The Gazooka"
"(That) Moment of Moments"
"Sentimental Weather"
"5 a.m."
"I Can't Get Started With You"
"Modernistic Moe"
"Dancing to Our Score"
Music by John McManus, Hans Spialek, Conrad Salinger, Russell Bennett, Don Walker.

Yokel Boy (1939-40) D: Lew Brown.
Judy Canova, Buddy Ebsen, Charles Althoff, Ann Canova, Zeke Canova, Dixie Dunbar, Lew Hearn, Jackie Heller, Ralph Holmes, Lois January, Ralph Riggs, Ben H. Roberts, Almira Sessions, Phil Silvers.
Opened on July 6.
Majestic Theatre (208 performances)

Musical comedy spoof of country folk and gangster films. Judy Canova plays Judy. Choreography by Gene Snyder.
Lew Brown-Charles Tobias-Sam H. Stept

Songs:
"Lem And Sue" performed by Judy Canova, Dunbar, Yokel Boys and Chorus
"I Know I'm Nobody"
"For The Sake Of Lexington" performed by entire cast
"Comes Love" performed by Judy Canova
"It's Me Again"
"Let's Make Memories Tonight"
"(Time for) Jukin'" *(music by Walter Kent)* performed by Judy Canova
"Uncle Sam's Lullaby"
"Hollywood and Vine"
"Catherine the Great" sung by Judy Canova and Royal Bodyguards
"The Ship Has Sailed"
"I Can't Afford to Dream"
"Lem and Sue" *(reprise)* performed by entire cast
"Comes Love" *(reprise)* performed by entire cast
"Uncle Sam's Lullaby" *(reprise)* performed by entire cast

No, No Nanette (1971)
Judy Canova.
National Touring Company

Musical comedy about a girl out to save her uncle from gold-diggers.

Television

Title Unknown (NBC, Experimental) May 3, 1939.
The Canovas [Judy, Ann, Zeke] do a hillbilly act for early television cameras.

Cavalcade of Stars (DuMont) September 26, 1952.
Host/Star: Larry Storch. The Sammy Spear/Charlie Spear Orchestra.
Live variety with singer-comedienne Judy Canova, songstress Mary Mayo and vocalist Don Richards. *Final show of the series.*

The Colgate Comedy Hour (NBC) November 2, 1952.
Host: Judy Canova. *Announcer:* John Cannon. The Charles Dant Orchestra.
Judy joins her siblings Ann and Zeke in a reunion of The Canovas — their skit is "Jesse James." Country gal Judy has a humorous encounter with refined Zsa

Zsa Gabor in a Pullman train berth. Judy takes a screen test and presents the skit "Maw and Paw." Other guests include singers Vic Damone and Carl Ravazza; pianist Liberace; actors Cesar Romero and Hans Conried; The Lancers. *Song:* "Dark Eyes" sung by Judy, Liberace.

Art Linkletter's House Party (CBS) March 10, 1954.
Host: Art Linkletter.
Daytime variety with guest Judy Canova.

What's My Line? (CBS) July 18, 1954.
Host: John Daly. *Panel:* Dorothy Kilgallen, Steve Allen, Arlene Francis, Bennett Cerf. *Announcer:* Lee Vines.
Game show in which the panelists take turns asking yes-or-no questions to determine the occupation of each contestant. Judy Canova is the Mystery Guest.

The Swift Show Wagon (NBC) March 5, 1955.
Host: Horace Heidt.
Comedienne Judy Canova comes on board when the Show Wagon stops at her home town of Fort Lauderdale, FL. The guest list includes The Vagabonds and local talent.

Matinee Theater (NBC) "She's the One with the Funny Face" November 15, 1955.
Host: John Conte.
An entertainer zooms back to stardom on television because of her homely appearance.

The Red Skelton Show (CBS) March 27, 1956.
Star: Red Skelton. *Announcer:* Art Gilmore. The David Rose Orchestra.
Guest Judy Canova joins Red in a sketch about a bitter mountain feud between the Kadiddlehoppers and the Canovas. Clem Kadiddlehopper (Red) develops a fondness for Judy, complicating matters for the feuding clans.

The Ina Ray Hutton Show (NBC) July 4, 1956.
Stars: Ina Ray Hutton & Her All-Girl Band. *Comic/Musician:* Mickey Anderson. *Announcer:* Diane Brewster.
Ina Ray leads her distaff orchestra and stars in a half-hour of variety featuring guest entertainers — all women. Special guest for the initial telecast is comedienne Judy Canova, who sings "I Ain't Got Nobody." Ms. Hutton's

group includes Mickey Anderson (comic vocals, saxophone, clarinet, flute); Dee Dee Ball (piano, organ); Helen Smith (bass); Margaret Rinker (drums); Jane Davies (guitar); Harriet Blackburn (saxophone, conga drums); Judy Von Ever, Evie Howeth, Helen Wooley (all on saxophone, clarinet); Lois Cronin (trombone, vibraphone); Peggy Fairbanks, Helen Hammond, Zoe Ann Willy (all on trumpet). *Live from Hollywood. Debut show of the series.*

The Tony Bennett Show (NBC) September 8, 1956.
Star: Tony Bennett. Vocalists: The Spellbinders. The Frank Lewis Dancers. The Carl Hoff Orchestra. Guests include singer Connee Boswell, comedienne Judy Canova, vocal quartet The Diamonds and dancer Pegleg Bates. *Final show of the series.*

The Rosemary Clooney Show (Syndicated) 1957.
Star: Rosemary Clooney. *Vocalists:* The Hi-Los [Bob Morse, Clark Burrows, Gene Puerling, Bob Strasen]. The Nelson Riddle Orchestra.
Variety with guest Judy Canova.

The Steve Allen Show (NBC) October 27, 1957.
Stars: Steve Allen, Louis Nye, Don Knotts, Tom Poston. *Announcer:* Gene Rayburn. The Skitch Henderson Orchestra. Guests include William Bendix from TV's *The Life of Riley;* singers Janice Harper, Jerry Vale; comedy monologist Shelley Berman; drummers Art Blakey, Candy Candido, Bob Rosengarden. Judy Canova appears as a "country girl." Skits include "Crazy Shots"; a Sputnik panel discussion with Steve, Tom, Don, and Louis; "The Football Benchwarmers" with Steve and William. Also, a drum jam-session among Art, Candy, Bob, and Steve.

The Danny Thomas Show (CBS) "The Country Girl" March 17, 1958.
Stars: Danny Thomas, Marjorie Lord, Rusty Hamer, Sherry Jackson, Angela Cartwright, Amanda Randolph.
Danny and his pal Benny discover talented singer Elsie Hopple (Judy Canova) at a diner in the mountains. Elsie decides to accept Danny's offer of a spot in his show, but her decision almost wrecks her marriage.
Benny: Ben Lessy

The Big Record (CBS) May 21, 1958.
Host/Star: Patti Page. The Vic Schoen Orchestra.
Live musical showcase with guest vocalist Jo Stafford, comedienne-singer Judy Canova, and drummer Buddy Rich.

The Judy Canova Show (pilot, unaired) circa 1958.
A traveling carnival entertainer (Judy Canova) deals with life on the road.

Milton Berle Starring in the Kraft Music Hall (NBC) December 31, 1958.
Star: Milton Berle. *Announcer:* Ken Carpenter. The Billy May Orchestra.
Tonight's guests are Judy Canova and singer Tommy Sands. In a sketch, Judy
shows Milton how to celebrate New Year's Eve country style. *Telecast live
and in color from Hollywood.*

The Judy Canova Show (pilot, unaired) 1959.
Situation comedy about the owner (Judy Canova) of a diner in the Ozarks.

Alfred Hitchcock Presents (CBS) "Party Line" – May 29, 1960.
Host: Alfred Hitchcock.
Heyward Miller once tricked Helen Parch (Judy Canova) to give up her
party line call so he could phone his bookie. Later, Miller tries to interrupt
again saying his wife desperately needs a doctor — but this time Helen will
not give up the line. Miller's wife dies as a result and Heywood winds up in
jail after a petty theft. When he gets out, the ex-con widower swears revenge
on the ignorant Ms. Parch.
Heywood: Arch Johnson. *Sheriff Atkins:* Royal Dano. *Emma:* Ellen Corby.
Betty Nubbins: Gertrude Flynn. *Mrs. Gertrude Anderson:* Charity Grace. *Mr.
Maynard, the Grocer:* Ted Knight.

Here's Hollywood (NBC) March 30, 1962.
Hosts: Jack Linkletter, Helen O'Connell.
Actress Judy Canova is interviewed. Actress Gale Robbins takes viewers on
a tour of her home.

Vacation Playhouse (CBS) "Cap'n Ahab" – September 3, 1965.
A deceased sea captain bequeathed his home and fortune to his two nieces —
provided they care for his longtime companion Cap'n Ahab, a wise-cracking
parrot.
Tillie Meeks: Judy Canova. *Maggie Feeney:* Jaye P. Morgan. *Battersea, the
Housekeeper:* Don Porter. *Miss Langdon:* Francine York. *Emcee:* Eddie Quil-
lan. *Hardhat:* Larry Blake. *Chauffeur:* Tom Lound. *Cop:* Murray Hill. *Delivery
Boy:* Tommy Alende.
Unsuccessful pilot for a proposed series to star Canova, Morgan, and Porter.

Pistols 'n' Petticoats (CBS) "Daisy and the Gambler" – January 7, 1967.
Stars: Ann Sheridan, Douglas V. Fowley, Ruth McDevitt, Gary Vinson, Carole Wells.
Grandma Hanks (McDevitt) doesn't cotton to gun-wielding Daisy Frogg (Judy Canova), who finds Grandpa's mean disposition mighty attractive.
Cowhand: Harry Raybould. *Gambler:* Bill Oberlin. *Virgil Hoeffer:* Bob Lyons.

Pistols 'n' Petticoats (CBS) "The Golden Fleece" – February 11, 1967.
Stars: Ann Sheridan, Douglas V. Fowley, Ruth McDevitt, Gary Vinson, Carole Wells.
Con-man Jake Turner was all set to go straight after a hitch in prison, but he may revert to his old ways: a well-heeled Easterner has come shopping for a gold mine.
Turner: Pat Buttram. *Sadie:* Judy Canova. *Clif Ledbetter:* Philip Bourneuf. *Lafayette Ambrose:* George Neise. *Ernie:* Walker Edmiston. *Buster:* Jay Ripley. *Lenny:* Murray MacLeod.

Li'l Abner (pilot, NBC) September 5, 1967.
It seems the lovely charms of beautiful Daisy Mae (Jeannine Riley) has captivated no less than Senator Henry Cabbage Cod, who makes a special junket to Dogpatch to "investigate." Based on the comic strip by Al Capp.
Li'l Abner Yokum: Sammy Jackson. *Mammy Yokum:* Judy Canova. *Pappy Yokum:* Jerry Lester. *Marryin' Sam:* Larry Mann. *Henry Cabbage Cod:* Robert Reed. *Unsuccessful pilot for a proposed series to star Jackson, Canova, Lester, and Riley.*

Comedy Preview (ABC) "The Murdocks and the McClays" – September 2, 1970.
A tale of rival feuding clans who figure "hate ain't no good 'less it's likewise." Faced with a Romeo-and-Juliet dilemma among their offspring, the oldsters insist the youngsters learn to like dislikin' whether they like it or not.
Angus McClay: Dub Taylor. *Julianna McClay:* Kathy Davis. *Calvin Murdock:* Noah Beery, Jr. *Junior Murdock:* John Carson. *Ida Murdock:* Judy Canova. *Grandpa Murdock:* Bill [William] Fawcett. *Grandma Murdock:* Nydia Westman. *Sheriff Bates:* James Westerfield. *Turkey:* George C. Fisher. *Unsuccessful pilot for a proposed series.*

Love, American Style (ABC) "Love and the Unsteady Steady"/"Love and the Persistent Assistant"/"Love and the Last Joke"/"Love and the Clinical Problem"/"Love and the Eats Café" – November 9, 1973.

Stars: Barbara Minkus, Tracy Reed, Phyllis Davis, Jim Hampton, James A. Watson Jr., Jed Allan.

A teenage boy wonders what it would be like married to his girlfriend. The assistant to a stage hypnotist is in love with her boss, but the feelings are unrequited. A writing couple has to come up with a comedy script on their honeymoon. Fighting marrieds seek professional help. A salesman in a rural town tries to keep a local girl from marrying a no-good man.

Bert Convy, Brandon Cruz, Kristy McNichol, Joanie Summers, Melanie Baker, Michelle Riskas, Vicki Schreck, David Pollock, Ann B. Davis, Dwayne Hickman, Susan Sennett, Judy Carne, Rich Little, Dr. Joyce Brothers, Jerry Stiller, Anne Meara, Judy Canova, Stockard Channing, Bob Denver, George Lindsey, Bill Hicks, Al Dunlap, Bob Golden.

Police Woman (NBC) "The Beautiful Die Young" – September 20, 1974. *Stars:* Angie Dickinson, Earl Holliman, Ed Bernard, Charles Dierkop, Val Bisoglio.

A modeling agency owner lures teenage girls into Japanese white slavery and porn films. Sgt. Pepper Anderson (Dickinson) goes undercover to shut him down.

Ted Adrian: William Windom. *Debbie Sweet:* Kathleen Quinlan. *Bonnie June:* Karen Lamm. *Don:* Harvey Jason. *Cora:* Jean Byron. *Rex:* Antonio Fargas. *The Arky Lady, an upset mother:* Judy Canova. *Police Cadet:* Cathy Rigby.

The Love Boat (ABC) "The Captain's Captain"/"Hounded"/"Romance Roulette" – November 26, 1977. *Stars:* Gavin McLeod, Bernie Kopell, Fred Grandy, Ted Lange, Lauren Tewes.

Captain Stubing's father is on board and makes everyone anxious with his demands. A dog traps a passenger in his cabin. Three female friends use a shipboard game to meet men.

Merrill Stubing Sr.: Phil Silvers. *P.J.:* Judy Canova. *Donald M. Flanders:* Gary Burghoff. *Morton:* David Landsberg. *Frank:* Vincent Baggetta. *Toby Chapman:* Susan Heldfond. *Beth:* Joanna Kerns. *Regina Parker:* Jane Curtin. *Also:* Markus Parilo, Gina Sorell.

Dinah! (Syndicated) July 20, 1978. *Host:* Dinah Shore.

The guests include mother and daughter combinations: Zsa Zsa Gabor and Francesca Hilton; Judy and Diana Canova; Lee Grant and Dinah Manoff.

"The All-Star Salute to Mother's Day" (Special, NBC) May 10, 1981.
Hosts: Ed McMahon, Jayne Kennedy.
Variety show in which celebrity guests (including Judy Canova and her daughter Diana) appear to honor mothers everywhere.
Claude Akins, Melissa Sue Anderson, Foster Brooks, Dr. Joyce Brothers, Charlie Callas, David Copperfield, Jamie Lee Curtis, Bob Denver, Eva Gabor, Zsa Zsa Gabor, Bobbie Gentry, Shecky Greene, Michele Lee, Janet Leigh, Barbara Mandrell, Irlene Mandrell, Louise Mandrell, Yvette Mimieux, Jim Nabors, Donald O'Connor, Debbie Reynolds, Don Rickles, Ginger Rogers, Brooke Shields, Richard Simmons, Rip Taylor, Bobby Vinton, Anson Williams, Cindy Williams.

Sources

Books and Periodicals

The Alfred Hitchcock Presents Companion by Martin Grams, Jr., and Patrik Wikstrom, OTR Publishing, 2001.

Archives of the Airwaves, seven volumes, by Roger C. Paulson, BearManor Media, 2005-2007.

The Big Broadcast 1920-1950 by Frank Buxton and Bill Owen, Flare/Avon, 1973.

The Columbia Story by Clive Hirschhorn, Crown, 1989.

The Complete Actors' Television Credits, 1948-1988, Vol. 2: Actresses, 2nd edition by James Robert Parish and Vincent Terrace, Scarecrow Press, 1990.

The Complete Directory to Prime Time Network and Cable TV Shows, 1946-present, 8th edition by Tim Brooks and Earle Marsh, Ballantine Books, 2003.

Encyclopedia of American Radio, 1920-1960 by Luther F. Sies, McFarland, 2000.

The Encyclopedia of Daytime Television by Wesley Hyatt, Billboard/Watson-Guptill, 1997.

Experimental Television, Test Films, Pilots and Trial Series, 1925 through 1995 by Vincent Terrace, McFarland & Co., 1997.

Feature Films, 1940-1949 by Alan G. Fetrow, McFarland & Co., 1994.

Feature Films, 1950-1959 by Alan G. Fetrow, McFarland & Co., 1999.

Feature Films, 1960-69 by Harris M. Lentz III, McFarland & Co., 2001.

The Films of the Seventies by Marc Sigoloff, McFarland Classics, 1984.

The Golden Age of B Movies by Doug McClelland, Bonanza Books, 1981.

Halliwell's Film and Video Guide, 6th edition, by Leslie Halliwell, Charles Scribner's Sons, 1987.

Hollywood Song: The Complete Film & Musical Companion, three volumes, by Ken Bloom, Facts on File, 1995.

"Judy Canova, Queen of Corn," article by Charles Stumpf, *Films of the Golden Age* magazine, No. 12, Spring 1998.

Leonard Maltin's Classic Movie Guide, edited by Leonard Maltin, Plume, 2005.

The MGM Story by John Douglas Eames, Crown, 1982.

Memories of Radio by Dick Judge

The New, Revised Ultimate History of Network Radio Programming and Guide to All Circulating Shows by Jay Hickerson, 1997.

On the Air: The Encyclopedia of Old-Time Radio by John Dunning, Oxford University Press, 1998.

The Paramount Story by John Douglas Eames, Crown, 1985.

Performers' Television Credits, 1948-2000, Vol. 1: A-F, by David M. Inman, McFarland & Co., 2001.

Radio Programs, 1924-1984: A Catalog of Over 1800 Shows by Vincent Terrace, McFarland & Co., 1999.

Radio's Golden Years: The Encyclopedia of Radio Programs 1930-1960 by Vincent Terrace, A.S. Barnes & Co., Inc., 1981.

Radio Speakers by Jim Cox, McFarland & Co., 2007. *The Republic Pictures Checklist* by Len D. Martin, McFarland & Co., 1998.

Same Time...Same Station by Ron Lackmann, Facts on File, Inc., 1996. *Sound Films, 1927-1939* by Alan G. Fetrow, McFarland & Co., 1992.

Television Specials, 3,201 Entertainment Spectaculars, 1939-1993 by Vincent Terrace, McFarland & Co., 1995.

Television Variety Shows by David M. Inman, McFarland & Co., 2006.

Total Television, 4th edition, by Alex McNeil, Penguin Books, 1996. *TV Guide* magazine, various issues 1952 to 1971.

Unsold Television Pilots, 1955 through 1989 by Lee Goldberg, McFarland & Co., 1990.

Videohound's Cult Flicks & Trash Pics, edited by Carol Schwartz with Jim Olenski, Visible Ink Press, 2002.

Videohound's Golden Movie Retriever 2007, edited by Jim Craddock, Thomson-Gale, 2006.

Vitaphone Films by Roy Liebman, McFarland & Co., 2003.

Internet Sites

The Classic TV Archive: *www.geocities.com/TelevisionCity/stage/2950/index.html*

Epguides.Com: *www.epguides.com*

Internet Broadway Database: *www.ibdb.com*

Internet Movie Database: *www.imdb.com*

Jerry Haendiges Radio Logs: *www.otrsite.com*

Jim Davidson's Classic TV Info: *www.classictvinfo.com*

Old Time Radio Researchers Group: *www.otrr.org*

RadioGoldinex: *www.radiogoldindex.com*

Tobacco Documents: *www.tobaccodocuments.com*

TV.Com: *www.tv.com*

Index

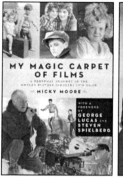

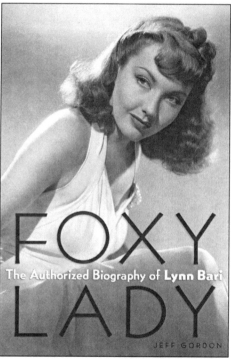

Breinigsville, PA USA
28 August 2010
244429BV00005B/4/P